A Few Choice Words

Carlton U. Forbes

A Collection of Inspirational and Motivational Discourses

CONTENTS

Preface

<u>A Few Choice Words</u> is more than a typical reading material. Instead, it is a collection of insightful discourses on a few select words, accompanied by compelling life lessons. Each entry contains a balanced mix of helpful and uplifting ideas to inspire every reader. The goal of this book is to present spirited and thoughtful discourses on matters of faith, virtues and other noteworthy ideas.

Undoubtedly, each entry will pique your interest; prompt you to ask valid questions, direct you to search reputable and trustworthy sources for the most compelling answers. In so doing, you will discover new truths that will enable you to understand your true purpose in life. This has been my experience in reading various literary sources, including the Scriptures, and seeking knowledge from above.

The presentations in this book were first given at the Samyook Language School, (a language training institute) in South Korea. Back then, I was actually working as an English teacher, employed by the North Chungcheong Office of Education. During that time, I often attended a local church near my school. Knowing that I was a former Samyook missionary-teacher, the coordinator and pastor often invited me to present the homily (non-doctrinal sermon) at their assembly and religious weekend programs. This was a normal routine for the missionary-teachers at Samyook Language Schools.

As a former Samyook missionary-teacher, I was often invited to speak with the students at various Branch Schools in South Korea. However, at that time, I thought it best to present select subject-matters without the normal preachy tone. Hence, I experimented with a more interactive style of engaging the students in meaningful discussions on various topics. Most often, I selected a word-theme, and used it as the launch-pad for an audience-centered dialogue.

Since the first presentation elicited encouraging responses from the students, I decided to select related word-themes, reflected on their meanings and merge them with applicable lessons. Then, after a contemplative and prayerful review, I wrote the script for my presentations. With each invitation, other word-themes were examined and interpreted with a biblical perspective. Soon, a growing collection was being assembled. After the seventh invitation, it became apparent that those scripts could be arranged into a single unit for a book. Although some editing of the original speeches was necessary, the central points and overall themes are identical to the original presentation shared in Cheonog-ju.

Now that A Few Choice Words has evolved into an actual publication, it is my hope that readers will gain valuable lessons with practical applications for their personal needs. My hope and prayer is that the message in each entry will positively affect the mind of every reader. That way, this book will prove its worth as an enlightening, edifying and uplifting reading experience. May God's richest blessings be yours, now and always!

Carlton U. Forbes

ACKNOWLEDGEMENTS

I gratefully acknowledge the encouragement of the following people whose collective support provided much of the impetus needed to make <u>A Few Choice Words</u> a reality. First on the list is my wife Wanda, who, after returning to the US, took charge of the household and the care of our three boys. Her devotion and commitment to me and our family provided both the encouragement and understanding I needed to undertake this literary endeavor. Also, the kindness and supportive friendship of Bae and Han Hyun Sook afforded me a suitable environment for harnessing the creative energies to write this book.

No less important are my three sons Carver, Jarvis, and Carson. They spur me on to use my time wisely to ensure my full attention will be theirs when they need it most. Next is my mom Vinel Johnson. She has taught me that fortune favors those who dare to dream and make sincere efforts to turn their dreams into reality. Also, the tips and suggestions of Veshta Ross, Amy Altman, and Carla Spence have helped immensely with revising the manuscript.

The motivation and assistance of the following people is also noteworthy: Teresa Williams, Makeba Mitchell, Pastor Soe Ho Deok, Chris and Mandy Mtsenga. It was in response to their invitation that the first entry in this collection was written. Their student-audiences were accommodating and considerate, courteous and very receptive every time I addressed them.

I cannot forget the encouragement of my sisters Marcia, and Nocole, or my brother Mark They help to make our family bond strong and supportive to every member. Also, my former college roommate Osane Garvey, and a host of others who make up the support network that inspires me to aim high, think big, and cherish my dreams.

Another person worth mentioning is Dr. Sylvia J. Barnes, my advanced composition professor in college. She was the first professor who urged me to write down some of my bright ideas in hopes of getting them published someday. Next is Professor Michaels, who taught me freshman composition. Her guidance and encouragement boosted my confidence to develop my writing skills, long after her coursework and assigned writing tasks were completed.

Equally important is Dr. Cecily A. Daly; whose caring support was my wellspring of courage and tenacity. Her wealth of constructive criticism and helpful advice continue to influence me in positive ways. Two other people worth mentioning are Drs. Dwain & Charmaine Woode— my best friends and stalwart patrons. Next are Dennis and Lloyda Williamson, whose friendship and insightful counsel is a source of strength and reassurance in my life.

Carlton U. Forbes

Foreword

As I type this word "Foreword," it occurs to me that the homophonic equivalent 'forward' is what Carlton Forbes is striving for in his own life, and that of his readers. Real life seldom follows the norms of the status quo. It is always in motion and perhaps we perceive it as moving up or down, forward or backward, or possibly, from one lateral position to another.

Wherever it is that we see ourselves in the ever-evolving process of gravitating from today into tomorrow, and leaving our yesterdays behind us, the fact is, we all want to move forward. We all dread the moment when it's apparent, we may have lost ground. Why? That's because to stand still is to become stale, stagnant and spiritless.

It's true that we all measure "forward" in varying ways. Some have an economic yardstick, while others may use an educational plumb line. Still others may regard social prominence or physical prowess as the barometer of their aptitude and attitude. I suppose the ability to use the guiding principles of one's forefathers to shape the ideas of others might be included in such a spectrum of gauges.

What Carlton Forbes has done in A Few Choice Words is open his mind and heart to his readers in an effort to share what life's experience, and a naturally inquisitive nature have shown him in his quest forward. I'm certain that he joins me in trusting your journey forward will be facilitated by this effort.

Charles (Chuck) L. Woods

Pastor - Olive Branch, MS.

A Few Choice Words

For more information, please visit my website:
http://carltonesl.com

Abundant Living

Introduction

<u>Opening Questions</u>

Is there anything you would like to have more of? What is one thing you consider most desirable? Is it your favorite food, designer fashion goods, jewelry or money? Can you recall a time in your life when you had an abundance of something you value or treasure? During the next few minutes, we'll examine the phrase "abundant living," and consider what it means to live an abundant life.

Reality teaches us that life is an experience that often requires taking the tests first, and learning the lessons afterwards. Despite the above premise, some of life's lessons can be learned without reliving the unpleasant experiences of others. How so? Well, collective knowledge informs us that individual actions and purposeful decision-making can militate against repeating known mistakes made by others and avoiding unwanted consequences. Fortunately, some people have the capability and capacity to alter their life circumstances. Sadly, that is not the case for millions, especially those born in conflict-ridden, undeveloped countries. This is especially true for those governed by kleptocrats, who use the nations' resources and wealth to benefit themselves and their corrupt cronies.

1

Hence, in the minds of many, life is like a game of chance. The lucky few seem to be on an unending winning streak. Such fortunate folks tend to have an abundance of accomplishments, progress and prosperity, high social status, and other trappings of success. Meanwhile, the unlucky multitude must deal with difficulties, cope with recurring disappointments, and endure a lifetime of struggles.

Knowing this, philosophers and great thinkers tend to devise summary statements on "life" that are worth contemplating. One commentator says "Life is like a long journey on unpaved roads, with winding paths and treacherous terrains." Oftentimes, the passage to our destiny is hazardous, long, and tiresome for so many of us. Again, the fortunate few have apparently acquired a reliable map or tour-guide; while the unfortunate mass must rely on grit and inner drive to reach their safe haven.

Life Summary Statements

Since mankind first became aware of their reasoning power, people have been summing up life with enlightening and insightful statements. The following reflects a choice collection of axioms on life. "Life is like a beautiful melody. Only the lyrics (words) are messed up"—Hans Christian Anderson.

"Life is what you make it; always has been, always will be"— Grandma Moses. "Life is like a mirror. If you frown at it, it frowns back. If you smile at it, it returns the greeting"— William Makepeace Thackeray. Reportedly, Forest Gump's Mother always says, "Life is like a box of chocolates. You never know what you're going to get."

With that in mind, I can hardly resist offering my own thoughts on the matter. Life is like a blank canvas. You have to risk making a mess to create great art. An alternative perspective is, life is like a picnic. You'll enjoy it better if you bring along lots of goodies.

Life is like a circus. The performances are more enjoyable when they are well-planned and perfectly executed. Despite the uncertainties of life, our experiences tend to be more meaningful when we play active roles in directing, engaging and pursuing purposeful goals. This means, those who are detached or indifferent towards their own wellbeing are more likely to feel disappointed and unfulfilled.

Defining Abundant

Most dictionaries define 'abundant' as a great quantity of something like a valuable commodity, a product available in large amounts; an ample, plentiful or sufficient supply of something. *Abundant* is an adjective. *Abundance* is a noun, and *abundantly* is an adverb. Synonyms of abundant are *bountiful*, *generous*, and *plenteous*, etc. (http://www.dictionary.com/)

Now, some may be tempted to ask, how can life be abundant if we only get to live it once? Well, such a query should be resolved by the end of this discourse. Until then, let's consider the following.

Farms that get the right balance of nutrients, sunshine and water usually yield an abundant harvest. Fields of barley, corn, oat, rice or wheat that receive the early spring rains tend to produce grains in abundance (bumper crop). Vines that are sufficiently nurtured and pruned tend to bear bountiful clusters of juicy, sweet grapes or berries.

Abundant Living

Naturally, farmers who are blessed with abundant harvests can gather enough provisions to feed their families and sell some in the market places. Families that are well-fed and cared for are more likely to be contented and satisfied with their lives. Naturally, such a favorable circumstance can create the conditions for contentment—an obvious indicator of abundant living.

Having an abundance of the things we value most is one of the obvious markers for living the good life. Similarly, earning enough income to obtain basic necessities as well as choice luxuries is one of the signs of prosperity. Those who are able to eat three balanced-meals daily, and enjoy some material comforts can be thought of as living well. The ability to provide for one's needs, and enjoy leisure activities and pleasurable indulgences is one of the benefits

4

of financial comfort, prosperity and a satisfying quality of life.

Scarcity and Want

Consider this! From the beginning, it was God's desire that mankind would enjoy abundant living forever. That's why He placed the first couple in paradise. The Garden of Eden had everything to meet their daily needs. However, shortly after sin became a reality, mankind began to experience scarcity and want. Consequently, tilling the soil became a necessity to produce foods for the growing needs of the first family. (Gen. 3:17-23)

Other consequences of sin are adverse ecological changes, political and social upheavals that make the world much different from the paradise-home God gave Adam and Eve. Despite advancements in agricultural science, everyday, millions of people battle hunger and struggle to feed themselves and their families, due to drought, famine and poverty. In many third-world or undeveloped countries, displaced and distressed populations are forced to survive on just one meal a day.

According to the World Food Organization, about 25,000 people die of hunger-related causes daily. The HungerProject.org estimates that up to 925 million people around the world lack the capacity to obtain enough food to meet their daily nutritional needs. Meanwhile, approximately 80% of the world's wealth and economic resources are controlled by just 2% of the population.

While affluent nations consume more than half the world's resources, one-third of the world's population is denied clean drinking water, basic nutrition, and adequate housing. Those who happen to live in war-torn countries and drought-stricken regions may live and die without ever encountering anything in abundance but poverty and want. Every day, they must cope with deprivation, malnutrition, and starvation. For some, life is just an empty existence, lacking in meaning, promise or purpose. Hence, given the chance, many willingly risk life and limb migrating to countries far or near; embarking on desperate quests in hopes of improving their lot in life.

Divine Blessings

Incidentally, this was not God's original plan for humanity. Instead, it was the Lord's desire that every person would have enough to meet their needs, so no one would be in want. However, the devil despises God, and seeks to destroy his created beings. Furthermore, Satan uses man-made and natural disasters like droughts, earthquakes, floods and wars to deprive mankind of his divine blessings. (1 Peter 5:8) Like a burglar, who breaks into homes when the owner least expects, the devil aims to steal our blessings, deprive us of our divine favors, and rob us of our God-given heritage. (John 10:10)

Nevertheless, God has not given up on the human race. He longs for us to experience the kind of abundance that Adam and Eve once enjoyed in Eden. And His only condition is our obedience to His words. God made this abundantly clear when declaring His intentions towards His people through Moses.

> If you fully obey the Lord your God and carefully follow all his commands I give you today, the Lord your God will set you high above all the nations on earth. All these blessings will come upon you. You will be blessed in the city and blessed in the country. The fruit of your womb will be blessed, and the crops of your land and the young of your livestock—the calves of your herds and the lambs of your flocks. Your basket and your kneading trough will be blessed. You will be blessed when you come in and blessed when you go out. The Lord will grant you **abundant prosperity**—in the fruit of your womb, the young of your livestock, and the crops of your ground—in the land he swore to your forefathers to give you. The Lord will open the heavens, the storehouse of his bounty; to send rain in due season and to bless all the work of your hands. You will lend to many nations, but will borrow from none."—Deut. 28:1-11—*New International Version*

The prophet Jeremiah shares another perspective on God's idea of abundance. "And I will fill to the full the soul of the priests with abundance, and my people shall be satisfied with my goodness, says the LORD."–Jer. 31:14–*King James 2000 Bible*

Life At Its Best

Like a malicious spiteful feign, Satan wants us to have a meaningless existence. Thankfully, God wants us to live life to the full. Even now, God wants us to experience abundant living. This reminds me of a statement made by Jesus. "I've come that you may have life, and have it more **abundantly**." (John 10:10) *King James 2000 Bible*

This means, Christ came to offer us fuller, richer and more satisfying lives. Naturally, an enriching life experience includes the blessings of **abundant living**. Indeed, abundant living is one of the conditions for life at its best. That is what God is offering to every believer today.

Now, the question is, "How can we experience **abundance** in a world of scarcity and want?" Simple! Like Enoch, we must walk with God in deeds, thoughts, and words. Like Job, we must hate evil, shun sin, and practice holy living. Like Joseph, we must abhor immorality, even at the risk of losing our favored status and suffering career setback. Like Daniel, we must purpose in our hearts to live above reproach, so our just and upright lives will inspire admiration even among our enemies.

Naturally, having such a noble and virtuous resolve requires us to know God's loving intentions towards us from his holy words. This will enable us to learn the lessons He has taught us, put His teachings into practice, and seek to please him with our lives. Like Abraham, our belief in God's promises will bolster our faith, imbue us with the audacity to stake our claims on the promises of scripture. Gradually, our maturing faith and trust will enable us to selflessly commit ourselves to the service of God and man. Then, God will reward us for our faith; he will bless us beyond measure, and grant unto us the heritage of Jacob. God's providence is brimming with abundance. And it is his good pleasure to give us abundant blessings. It is high time for every sincere believer to experience physical and spiritual abundance in their lives.

How to Obtain Abundance

Do you want to experience the abundant life God offers? Then take Jesus at his word; put your trust in him. Pray earnestly and fervently for God's abundant blessings, and you will receive heaven's bountiful endowments.

Like Jabez, we too must acknowledge our need, convey with fervor our desires, and tell God specifically what we want Him to do for us. As our kindhearted father, God stands ready to expand our territories, and extend His providential care over us. (1 Chron. 4:9-10)

While still a youthful king, the Lord appeared unto Solomon in a vision. The Lord said to him, "Ask what I shall give you." The Scripture tells us that Solomon asked "for an understanding heart, so he could judge his people wisely, and discern between good and bad." The Lord was so pleased with Solomon's request, He granted unto him an understanding heart, fame, honor, and riches in abundance.

Like Solomon, we too must earnestly seek divine favors, and petition the Gracious Giver for heaven's choicest gifts. We too must pray for wisdom so we can differentiate between good and evil, right and wrong. That's a sure way to obtain divine guidance to help us make wise choices throughout our lives. (1 Kings 3:5-14).

When we live our lives in harmony with God's will, He will give us his **abundant** blessings. The Apostle Paul's assertion is a fitting affirmation here. "And God is able to bless you abundantly, so that in all things at all times, having all that you need, you will abound in every good work" (2 Cor. 9:8).

Conclusion

Dear reader! From the beginning, it was God's desire to fill your life with bounty, not scarcity. As believers, the time is right for God's people to start living life at its best. Even now, God wants to give us heaven's best blessings bountifully, not stingily. God longs for us to live in prosperity, not poverty; to experience His sufficiency, not bankruptcy.

Our heavenly father wants us to enjoy good health, a fortunate circumstance, His sufficient grace, and an abundance of heavenly gifts. After all, heaven is a place of affluence, luxury and opulence. And before we get there, God wants to give us a foretaste of what's to come.

Christ's admonition to His disciples is applicable for us today. "Ask and it shall be given you. Seek and you shall find. Knock and it shall be open unto you" (Luke 11:9). Even now, God wants you, me and all his children to enjoy a fuller, richer, and more satisfying life—**abundant living**.

The Last Word!

As the apostle Paul assures us, "Now to him who is able to do far more **abundantly** than all that we ask or think, according to the power at work within us… Amen." (Eph. 3:20)—ESV)

Let us pray.

Heavenly Father! Thank you for your loving intentions toward us; for the reminder that you want us to experience abundant living. Lord, we long to live life at its best, to have fuller, richer and more satisfying lives.

11

Give us willing hearts to follow your instructions and live our lives in accordance with your divine will. Grant unto us your choice blessings, and the bountiful gifts of heaven. We ask these favors in Jesus' name, amen.

Remedy for Anxiety

Introduction

<u>Emotional Beings</u>

It is said that humans are emotional beings. That's because we are so easily influenced by our emotions. Oftentimes, our emotions affect our actions, guide our decisions, and shape our attitudes. Other times, our emotions may even influence our temperament, making us more susceptible to certain ideologies and religious views. Hence, people who are easily affected by emotionally charged stimuli are more susceptible to brainwashing and suppressive indoctrination.

Thanks to normal emotional triggers, we are able to feel hopeful, joyful, and even sorrowful, based on our personal circumstances. Similarly, our emotions can also evoke feelings of gladness and sadness, depending on the changing conditions we experience. Conversely, the accompanying distress caused by emotional disorders can also lead to madness. This is especially true when madness is a consequence of an overwhelming emotional traumas like calamities or catastrophes, misfortunes and tragedies that leave people with mental scars, forcing them to cope to cope with unspeakable loss.

No Emotions, No Virtue

Aided by our emotions, we can muster the resolve to pursue our ambitions with passion. However, emotional and irrational responses can also give rise to feelings of distress, helplessness and hopelessness. Still, without our emotions, we would have difficulties putting our faith into practice, building trust and responding to loving affections.

Additionally, there are times when our emotions can become the source of apprehension and tension. Most people, at some point in their lives, have felt anxious about someone or something. Moreover, feelings of anxiety, fear and worry are manifestations of our emotional response to uncertainties. Among the list of human emotions, anxiety can be regarded as a frequent and potent stress-trigger. That is, anxiety is oftentimes, an obvious precursor to fear, stress, and uneasiness.

Defining Anxiety

Anxiety is defined as a feeling of fear, nervousness or tension; being apprehensive or uneasy about something— real or imagined. Synonyms of anxiety are *nervous-tension, unease, stress, worry, jitters*, etc. (http://www.dictionary.com/)

Generally, anxiety is a natural emotional response triggered by challenging, dangerous or frightening experiences. For example, a difficult test, an important assignment, public presentation or a new project can make us feel overly anxious. That's because, as humans, we are prone to worry about the unknown, risks of failure, and 'what ifs...' Also, acute anxiety can be a physiological indicator of uncertainty and insecurity.

Anxiety-ridden

No doubt, most people are anxious about at least a few things in their lives. Many middle school students are anxious about making the transition to high-school, and eventually, college. High school students are anxious about doing well on those intimidating aptitude or college entrance exams.

Once they pass that grueling challenge, their feelings of jubilation and triumph is short-lived. Even after getting satisfactory scores, their elation is quickly overtaken by anxiety about gaining acceptance into top-ranking universities. Likewise, university seniors are anxious about their job prospects after graduation. Furthermore, office workers are anxious about their chances of getting promotions, annual bonuses and pay increases. Parents are anxious about the rising cost of educating their children. Athletes are anxious about their next big game, championship match or trophy tournament. Even coaches are anxious about their next performance-evaluation review, and prospect for favorable contract renewal terms.

Naturally, celebrities too are anxious about landing a 'leading or pivotal role' that can earn nominations for an Oscar, Golden Globe, and other coveted awards. Why? That's because such honors enhance their public and professional profile, bolstering their reputation in the performing arts; enabling them to project the kind of image that attract fans worldwide, and maintain their 'most popular status.'

Politicians too are equally anxious about crafting the kind of message that will rally their supporters and increase their chances of winning their next elections. Voters are also anxious about their public representatives supporting sensible legislations that lead to national and personal prosperity. Even religious people are at times, anxious about adhering to the doctrines of their faith; performing their moral and sacred duty, practicing piety, and doing all that is necessary to ensure God's favor. Thankfully, heaven knows about the harsh realities that trigger our anxieties.

Anxiety Attack

Surprisingly, I too get anxiety-stricken almost every time I visit the doctor's office. Why? Well, doctors have a knack for prescribing injections as suitable treatment for certain medical conditions. Whenever I see that long, shiny needle, I get a mild case of anxiety attack. Actually, just seeing a nurse with a needle on TV makes me cringe.

An Anxiety-ridden Episode

This brings to mind an anxiety-ridden hospital visit I had
some years ago. One morning, while rushing down the
stairs in my apartment, I twisted my right ankle. At first, I
only felt a sharp pain in my joint, which lasted for a brief
moment. Feeling only a slight discomfort in my talus, I
went to work as usual. Throughout the day, I did all that
was required of me without any problems.

However, as evening came, and the stress from going up
and down the stairs began to affect my ankle, I started
feeling a twinge of pain in the affected area. Upon close
examination, it seemed slightly swollen; but no other signs
of anything serious. So I went home about 5:30 pm,
performed my evening chores, and even went cycling for
about thirty minutes after dinner.

After a long day of teaching and playing language games
with my students, I felt both exhausted and weary. So I
went to bed about 10:30 pm. To my dismay, before dozing
off, I felt a throbbing sensation in my ankle. Thinking that
a good night's rest would be healing therapy for my ankle,
the slight pain seemed like something I could ignore for the
sake of a sweet slumber. Sadly, I was mistaken.

Hours later, my sleep was interrupted by sharp, painful
sensations shooting through my lower leg. As the night
progressed, the pain got worse. Sometime after midnight,

the pain became so unbearable, I quickly talked myself into seeking medical attention.

Reluctantly, I stumbled out of bed, hobbled down the stairs, dragged myself into my car, and drove to the nearest hospital. Within minutes, I pulled into the nearby university hospital parking lot, and hopped on one leg, into the emergency room. Since the intake clerk did not speak English, she could not understand my answers to her questions. Hoping to speed up the paperwork procedure, she took my ID and insurance cards, and handed me a form, indicated where I should write my name at the top, and sign at the bottom. I hastily scribbled my name in the required slots and raised my ankle while sitting in the wheelchair delivered to me.

One nurse wheeled me into the main treatment galley where I waited, writhing in pain for what seemed like a long pause in the passage of time. Shortly after, another nurse came by, and asked the customary questions. Without even waiting to hear my answers, she grabbed my ankle and squeezed it in the epicenter of the pain. Since she was noticeably cute, I didn't want to cry in her presence. So I moaned in muffled tones.

Another long waiting period passed before the doctor showed up. He did the same thing as the nurse, and recommended x-ray. After examining the x-ray, he told me "There is no fracture, just a sprain." So he prescribed anti-inflammatory pain medication via injection. Soon, the nurse returned, swabbed my left arm, and shoved a long, probing needle into my small vein. To both our disappointment, that vein immediately collapsed. Without hesitation, she started eyeing my right arm.

At that point, I offered a suggestion. "Just give me the injection in my hind region and be done with it!" Regretfully, my suggestion was ignored, and her cute smile made me comply with her wishes. Reluctantly, I gave her my right arm. Again, she swabbed the spot chosen for the intrusive jab, shoved another long, probing needle into my small vein. Regrettably, that vein too collapsed.

Seeing that I was injected twice, with no satisfactory results, her cute smile lost its charm on me. I urged her to just administer the injection in my rump and put an end to my torturous ordeal. Instead, she seemed determined to ignore my pleas and started eyeing my left arm again.

Feeling manipulated by a cute nurse, I told her "I want to go home." She replied, "But you came here because of the pain in your ankle." "Yes," I responded, "but now, I have a pain in my ankle, my left and right arms too. So my condition is getting worse, not better!"

Apparently, the tone of my voice, my anguished pleas and stern stance made her call the doctor. He returned momentarily, and after the nurse explained the situation to him, he tried to give me a pep-talk about "taking it like a man." I insisted, "I'll do just that if the shot could be administered to one of my hind-cheeks. No more failed attempts to coax an uncooperative vein!" He eventually relented, and my anxiety-ridden episode ended with a slight intrusive puncture on my gluteus maximus. Moments later, my pain began to subside. Eventually, I returned home and slept contentedly.

Thankfully, since that time, I have not had a reason to visit that hospital again. That experience has also caused me to take extra care when going up or down stairs. The mere thought of having to relive that tortuous episode is all the reason I need to watch my steps. Even if I never have another sprained ankle, that anxiety-ridden hospital visit will not be easily forgotten.

Unfortunately, for most people, anxiety-ridden episodes are not so easily resolved. Nevertheless, God is concerned about the negative ways anxiety afflicts us. So the Lord has put in place remedies for our anxieties. As the apostle Peter admonishes us, "Cast all your anxieties on the Lord, he cares for you." (Psalms 55:22; 1Peter 5:7)

A Sports Analogy

In case you are wondering how to apply this text in practical ways, let me use a sports analogy. In soccer, star players like Cristiano Renaldo, Lionel Messi, and Samuel Eto'o are known for their abilities to butt, bump or kick the ball into the goal pen.

Incidentally, their opponents know this. So they do their utmost to keep the ball away from these star scorers. Fortunately, their teammates are instructed to get control of the ball and pass it to the star players. During the game, each player passes the ball closer to the goal pen, until finally, the star player kicks it in and scores.

The Teamwork Tactic

The same strategy is equally effective in basketball. Michael Jordan is indeed the greatest basketball player of all time. Still, he has never won a game by himself. Instead, he and his teammates strategize to setup power-plays in hopes of gaining a winning-edge over their opponents.

So with tactical teamwork, Michael Jordan often succeed in outscoring his rivals. Like Michael Jordan, Beckhem and Renaldo, God wants to use his expertise and specialized skills in helping us gain advantages in life. As your Team Captain, the Lord has a winning strategy for life's most important games.

Divine Tactics and Strategies

The same is true in our daily struggle with life's challenges. Regardless of your apprehension, fear or nervous-tension, with Christ as your Team Captain, you can count on a winning strategy for life's most important games. Every day, our Lord says to us, "Give me your anxieties, your cares, your fears, and your worries."

Whenever life's challenges assail you with nervous-tension, remember this. God is ready to help you with the most effective strategies to overcome your anxieties. Even now, he is saying to you: "I will empower you; I will devise the power-plays to help you outscore, outsmart and outwit your opponents. I will assist you with winning tactics. I will aid your advancement in the job-market, company boardroom and career field."

Conclusion

Do you need help managing your anxieties? Then God's teamwork tactic is your effective strategy. Even now, the Lord is saying to you, 'I will help you manage your stress, endure your struggles, and meet your challenges with courage. I will help you deal with life's harsh realities, overcome your obstacles, and gain the winning edge to succeed. Even better, I will relieve your troubled mind, I will enable and empower you; and will soothe your soul with solace.'

Why? That's because God is your freehanded Father; he loves you unreservedly and wholeheartedly. The wealth of the world is at His disposal. Indeed, our Heavenly Father is eager to supply our needs, and ensure our mental, physical and spiritual wellbeing. That's because being our compassionate, considerate and kindhearted caretaker is His good pleasure.

Like the Psalmist, you too can place your confidence in this reassuring pledge. "4Delight yourself in the LORD; And he will give you the desires of your heart. 5Commit your way to the LORD, Trust also in him, and he will do it." (Psalm 37:4&5) NASV

The Last Word!

"Cast all your anxiety on him because he cares for you." (1 Peter 5:7)

Let us Pray.

Heavenly Father! Thank you for your loving-kindness towards us; for offering to relieve our anxieties, stress and worries. Lord, we know it's not practical to live an anxiety-free life. So enable us to sharpen our coping skills so we can minimize the adverse effects of every anxiety-ridden episode.

Teach us how to trust in your teamwork tactic, and specialized strategies. Enable us to gain the winning edge in the race of life. Empower us to manage our anxieties, so we'll be able to live more fulfilling, healthier and happier lives. We ask these favors in Jesus name, amen,

Attitude Matters

Introduction

<u>Opening Questions</u>

In your opinion, what is attitude? Do you think of yourself as someone with a good attitude? Do you know someone who has a bad attitude? Which do you think is more beneficial: a good or bad attitude?

<u>Responses to Life's Events</u>

Attitude is a word often used to describe our behavior, feelings and responses to life's events. Most often, a cheerful, easy-going, happy-go-lucky person is thought of as having "a good attitude." Conversely, a complaining, disagreeable, and grumpy person is believed to have "a bad attitude."

If you react calmly to a chaotic or stressful situation, one might say "you have a good attitude." If you are often angry, irritable and mean-spirited for no good reason, then your friends will probably say, "You have a bad attitude." They may not tell you this to your face; but are probably thinking it, and may even share that sentiment with others. If you are aloof, iffy or indecisive, indifferent towards events happening around you, then you could be accused of having "a passive attitude—a dispassionate demeanor." Also, a person who acts inappropriately, annoys friends and

24

loved-ones, causes others to avoid his/her company, could be advised to "change his/her attitude."

<u>Attitudes and Daily Decisions</u>

Attitude is a character-trait (mindset) that can be good, bad or neutral. In fact, our attitudes can be shaped by our environment, religious beliefs, parental upbringing and social norms. Attitude is not permanently set or genetically fused into our being. Instead, it can be changed for better or worse—based on the decisions we make every day.

Defining Attitude

Dictionary.com <u>defines</u> attitude as a feeling or emotional response to life's events, one's disposition, manner or mindset towards everyday circumstance. It is an orientation or tendency to react in certain ways that are characteristic to one's personality. Synonyms of attitude are *demeanor, disposition, frame of mind, inclination, point-of-view or perspective*. Word Usage: *attitude* is a noun, and *attitudinal* is an adjective. Knowing this, the following thoughts on attitude are worth pondering.

Quotable Quotes

The renown transformational coach, Malgorzata Chabrowska, asserts that "<u>Attitude</u> is a person's inner thoughts and feelings." <u>Sir Winston Churchill</u> contends that "Attitude is a little thing that makes a big difference."

Thomas Jefferson insists that "Nothing on earth can stop the man with the right attitude from achieving his goals. Nothing on earth can help the man with the wrong mental attitude."

Charles R. Swindoll, the renown preacher, hints at the pivotal role attitude plays in our lives. "I am convinced that life is 10% what happens to me and 90% how I react to it. And so it is with you; you are in charge of your attitude." "I can't change the direction of the wind, but I can adjust my sail to reach my destination"—Jimmy Dean. "If you don't like something, change it. If you can't change it, then change your attitude"—Maya Angelou. "The greatest discovery of all time is that a person can change his future by merely changing his attitude"—Oprah Winfrey.

Changing and Shaping our Attitudes

Attitude is the mindset that engenders courage, spurs purposeful action, and stirs determination. Life is what happens to us. Circumstance is what surrounds us. Attitude is what shapes our point-of-view. Attitude guides our behavior, impacts on our morals and inspires change that matters. Indeed, a positive attitude sets our mental gears in motion to produce positive results.

A Good Attitude

As you can see, a good attitude is like a charming personality. It makes a disagreeable person more agreeable and likable. A good attitude makes a grumpy person good-natured and warm-hearted.

A good attitude turns feelings of despondency into cheerfulness and hopefulness. It can make a pessimistic person more confident and optimistic. With a good attitude, challenges can be changed into possibilities, obstacles into steppingstones, madness into gladness, certain failures into unexpected successes, and misfortunes into golden opportunities.

A Passive Attitude

Indeed, there are times when a passive attitude may seem like harmless indifference. However, when left unchecked, passivity can easily turn to apathy, which is neither helpful nor innocent. Instead, it is symptomatic of a more serious problem—hidden hostility masquerading as passivity. Even worse, an overly passive person often has difficulty seeing the value in improving him or herself. Consequently, people who have no vested interest in their wellbeing are often content with a passive attitude. Actually, a person with a passive attitude is oftentimes, unaffected by the hopeful, positive things that occur each day. Eventually, such detached indifference will likely morph into contempt—precluding a positive attitudinal change.

A Bad Attitude

The truth is, a bad attitude is not only undesirable, if it remains unchanged, it can ultimately leads to self-destructive behaviors and habits. Armed with a bad attitude, even sensible people are susceptible to doing senseless things. Have you ever wondered why some seemingly smart people tend to make such dumb decisions? Quite possibly, a bad attitude is at the very heart of this mind-boggling muddle. Why? That's because a bad attitude is symptomatic of impaired judgment and unbalanced reasoning. Left unchecked, a bad attitude naturally leads to careless, reckless and thoughtless conduct. Doubtless, such rash indiscretions have led many smart people down the road to ruin.

It is the spirit of Satan that afflicts us with a bad attitude. Oftentimes, people with bad attitudes are also antagonistic towards God, His people, and the plan of salvation. The Bible contains numerous examples of individuals whose antagonism towards God and his people became a flashpoint for divine deliverance and intervention. The Pharaoh that reigned during the Biblical Exodus comes to mind as one ruler with a bad attitude.

Stubborn Disposition

Despite multiple plagues that caused ruinous results to his kingdom, and terrible suffering for his people, Pharaoh remained arrogant, indignant and stubborn. He and his people endured the bloody Nile, noisome frogs, hordes of lice and outbreak of pestilent flies. Additionally, the death of their cattle, boils, hail, hordes of locusts, and three days of pitch-darkness throughout the land, were the direct result of Pharoah's mulish obstinacy. Yet, the headstrong ruler remained unmoved and unwilling to do what God said. Only after the deathly plague that killed the firstborn of every Egyptian household, including the royal family, did he decide to let God's people go.

Astoundingly, just hours after letting Israel go, Pharaoh had a change of heart. Both he and his servants regretted giving in to Moses' demands. Haunted by the thought of losing their cost-free labor source, they decided to pursue the Hebrews in hopes of recapturing their former slaves. Under Pharaoh's command, the Egyptian Army caught up with the people at the Red Sea, and was only hindered by the peculiar pillars of cloud and fire. Strangely enough, when Pharaoh saw his labor force escaping through the dry seabed, he insisted on going in after them. Being blinded by arrogance and pride, he couldn't resist pursuing them, at the risk of his own doom (Ex. 5-12). Alas, his bad attitude made it difficult for him to acknowledge that he couldn't fight against the Almighty God and win.

A Haughty Attitude

Another person with a royally bad attitude was Queen Jezebel. Due to Israel's worship of idols and strange deities, God allowed a famine to ravage the land for three and a half years. After being summoned by Elijah on Mount Carmel, Jezebel's soothsayers were exposed as phony prophets, and executed. Then, in the showdown on Mount Carmel, Elijah prayed for a divine rain-shower to end the long drought.

When King Ahab told Jezebel what Elijah had done, she was livid. She wrote an angry letter, with a royal threat to murder God's prophet within 24 hours. Queen Jezebel did not care about the famine's adverse impact on her people, nor did she care to acknowledge the rain shower summoned by Elijah to end the drought. Instead, she was furiously fervent with her single-minded purpose; misuse the state's power to terrorize the man of God. (1 Kings 19:1-2) Hence, Elijah's flight from the reach of her henchmen made him the first person in history to be "jezebelized"— scared by a Jezebel.

Arrogant Nobleman

King Xerxes' Chief of Staff, Haman, is another high profile person whose bad attitude caused his eventual downfall. The book of Esther tells us, Mordecai was just a lowly courtier in Xerxes' Court. Customarily, most courtiers showed their respect for the king and his royal officials, by bowing to them. However, Mordecai objected to that practice on account of his religious beliefs. Though it is understandable why such an objection would have bothered Haman, still, it was obvious, Mordecai was just a low ranking officer. Yet, Haman was so annoyed by Mordecai's 'conscientious objection,' he became arrogant, indignant and obsessive.

Being overly fixated with coercing everyone to pay him homage, Haman decided to make an example of Mordecai. Apparently, Haman felt justified in abusing his royal authority to get the honor he craved. First, he tried courtly enforcement with the humble courtier. When that effort failed, his prideful obsession led him to willfully conspire against Mordecai and his family. Alas, Haman concocted a plan to surreptitiously hoodwinked Xerxes into issuing an edict, decreeing the annihilation of a harmless group of people, most of whom he had never met, who posed no threat to himself or his family. Such a sinister scheme was merely a cover for branding Mordecai an 'enemy of the state.'

Unable to restrain his malicious intentions, Haman obtained the king's seal under false pretense, used it to enact an evil edict, commanding the execution of Mordecai, and his family. Wanting to make sure no one else would dare refuse him reverence, Haman's plot also sanctioned the slaughter of anyone else in the kingdom with similar objections, religious or otherwise. Unbeknownst to Haman, his plot had unwittingly ensnared Queen Esther, who was also a Jewess. When his pernicious plot was finally exposed, he lost his head on the very gallows he

ordered built for Mordecai's execution. (Est. 3-7) This
brings to mind one Biblical truism. "Pride goes before
destruction, and a haughty spirit before a ruinous crash."—
(Prov. 16:18) *King James 2000*

Jealousy Run-Amok

Throughout his ministry, Jesus had many encounters with
people who had bad attitudes. During one such encounter,
his enemies threatened to stone him. Why? Partly because
Jesus had insinuated that he was the Son of God. Even
worse, they also alleged that God's Begotten Son was
under the influence of Beelzebub.

Furthermore, they even called Him a glutton, "a Samaritan;
one possessed by a demon," and worse, a wine bibber.
They were confounded by the fact that Jesus had no
affiliation with the priestly and religious elites. Yet, he was
able to teach with authority, and performed so many
miracles. Hence, "...**the people were astonished at his
teachings:** 29For he taught them as one having authority,
and not as the scribes"—(Matthew 7:28,29). Employing
the use of colloquial appeals and simple parables, Jesus was
so effective in connecting with his audience, and engaging
them with his true-to-life stories, "… the common people
heard him gladly"—(Mark 12:37). Evidently, the ruling
elites' disdain for the itinerant teacher made them unwilling
to even consider the possibility that a folksy, lowly Rabi
could be the "Christ"—Promised Messiah.

Reacting to their antagonistic attitude, Jesus declared, "You are of your father the Devil, and his works you will do. He was a murderer from the beginning, and the father of lies." (John 8:39-44; John 10:27-39) Christ's divine indictment of his enemies shows that a bad attitude is the manifestation of evil influence spoiling our personality.

Indeed, it is the spirit of Satan that afflicts us with a bad attitude. Clearly, a bad attitude makes it more difficult to reach our full potential, to strive for greatness, to live productive and purposeful lives. As the above examples show, a bad attitude is a sign of devilish influence wreaking havoc on the individuals it controls. Thankfully, God has a plan to counteract the negative effects of a bad attitude.

Consider this!

Since we are all born into a world ravaged by the corrosive nature of sin, almost everyone will eventually need to make an attitude adjustment. Actually, the efforts to cultivate a good attitude necessitates a change, not only of our behavior and demeanor, but our mindset and thought-patterns as well. The Bible counsels us to seek divine aid when making an attitude adjustment. Knowing this, the following text adds divine validity to this viewpoint.

> "You, however, did not come to know Christ that way. Surely you heard of him and were taught in him in accordance with the truth that is in Jesus. You were taught with regard to your former way

of life, toput-off your old self, which is being corrupted by its deceitful desires; to be made new in the attitude of your minds; and to put on the new self, created to be like God in true righteousness and holiness." (Eph. 4:20-24)

Change in Attitude

Paul is telling us that a change in attitude may require a change in our thinking. This kind of change can only happen with divine assistance. Thankfully, God stands ready to assist us in changing our attitude from bad to good, from good to better, from better to noble.

As the following passage advises us, "Don't copy the behavior and customs of this world; but let God transform you into a new person by changing the way you think. Then you will learn to know God's will for you, which is good and pleasing and perfect." (Rom. 12:2).

Cultivating a Good Attitude

Now, the question is, how can you cultivate a good, positive, and wholesome attitude? Simple! First, ask yourself these questions. "Do I have a bad, good or passive attitude?" "What kind of attitude do I want to have?" Then, make up your mind to cultivate a new attitude—one that will bolster your image, and enhance your effectiveness in living your best life, while striving for the mastery.

34

Most importantly, ask God to give you the wisdom you need to make the kind of change that matters most. A change of attitude may require a change in habits, lifestyle, thinking and perspective. God will empower you with courage, and infuse you with focused-determination to improve yourself physically, mentally and spiritually. A good, positive, wholesome attitude will enhance your effectiveness in pursuing your endeavors, being more productive in your work, and obtaining meaningful progress in your quest for success.

Dear reader, helping you live your best life is God's good pleasure. A good attitude gives you added advantages for living up to your full potential. In so doing, you'll be empowered to pursue your life's goals, and ensure your plans encompass the fulfillment of heaven's purpose for you.

Conclusion

Clearly, there is nothing good about having a bad attitude. With a bad attitude, there is so much to lose, and little or nothing to gain. But with a good attitude, we put ourselves in a favorable circumstance for untold blessings and divine graces. Actually, a good attitude is like a godly quality that endears us to God and man, earth and heaven; prepares us for a promising future, and our eternal destiny.

The Last Word!

Finally brethren, whatever is true,
whatever is honorable, whatever is fair,
whatever is acceptable, whatever is
commendable, if there is anything of
excellence, and if there is anything
praiseworthy—keep thinking about
these things—(Phil. 4:8).

Let us pray.

Heavenly Father! It is good to know the advantages of a
cheerful, healthy attitude. Lord, we long to cultivate a
good, positive, wholesome attitude.

May your Holy Spirit endow us to develop an attitude of
gratitude! Empower us with your divine grace, and enable
us to change our mindset from bad to good, from good to
better, from better to noble. We ask these favors in Jesus'
name, amen.

Reason to Believe

Introduction

<u>Opening Questions</u>

I would like to begin this discussion by asking the following questions. Do you consider yourself a believer? If so, can you explain the benefits of being a believer? If per chance you are not a believer, how would you describe yourself—a nonbeliever, unbeliever or skeptic?

Now, please indulge my quizzical nature a bit longer. What does it mean to be a believer? Conversely, what does it mean to be a non-believer? Do non-believers believe in nothing? Do unbelievers doubt everything? Let's reexamine the concept of belief in hopes of answering the above questions.

<u>Life is Worth Living</u>

Life is an experience that is best enjoyed as a believer. From the moment we became aware of ourselves, we began to believe life is worth living. Initially, much of what we've come to believe started with assumptions. While in the womb, our conscious awareness of ourselves and surrounding started taking shape. Quite possibly, the intuitively perceptive 'embryonic self' can easily assume all is well with the world, and its future full of promise and possibilities.

Consider this!

During the nine months of gestation, the fetus learns to adapt to its surrounding. As the brain and other critical organs became more developed, the baby starts sensing an awareness of itself, its mother, familiar sounds and sensations. In time, it also learns to enjoy its' own company, by engaging in fetal play and acrobatics.

Then, about 260 days later, suddenly, without warning, the baby is rudely and traumatically evicted from its inner sanctum. Thankfully, the baby's memory of this traumatic experience is short-lived; and in time, most of its preconceived assumptions about life is confirmed. As the mother takes the child and cuddles it in her bosom, it finds solace in its acceptance and sense of belonging in the family. From the moment of its first suckling session, the infant's bond with its mother is reaffirmed. Soon, other beliefs about its new environment begins to take shape.

Fortunately, most babies are lucky enough to have caring and loving parents. Naturally, with nurturing affection and support, they learn to trust and depend upon their parents for sustenance, safety and security. As they grow from infancy into childhood, their belief-system is continually being shaped and redefined.

Life's Impact on Beliefs

During the transition from infancy to toddlerhood, childhood to adulthood, some children begin to recognize there is meaning and purpose for their lives. However, as life's changing fortunes become more impactful, unpleasant dramas and traumas may cause them to question long-held beliefs. Eventually, life's harsh realities begin to affect their belief-system in a major way. For some, occasional mishaps and missteps help strengthen their faith in what they believe. For others, distress and despair lead to erosion of their belief-system.

Defining Belief

Now, the reader may be wondering 'what exactly is belief, and how does it benefit me?' First, before answering that question, it seems prudent to consult a reputable dictionary. Belief is a confident feeling, a hopeful attitude about something; a feeling or sense of certainty that something is real, true or sure to happen. *Belief* is a noun, and *believe* is a verb. (http://www.dictionary.com/) Knowing this, the following thoughts on belief are worth pondering.

Quotable Quotes

One unknown writer shares the following tip. "Imagine with all your mind! Believe with all your heart! Achieve with all your might!"—Anonymous. "Just as much as we see in others, we have in ourselves"—William Hazlitt.

"All of us have wonders hidden in our breasts, only needing circumstances to evoke them"—Charles Dickens. "A person can grow only as much as his horizon allows"— John Powell. "All that Adam had, all that Caesar could, you have and can do.... Build, therefore, your own world!"—Ralph Waldo Emerson.

Innate Need to Believe

Some people believe in luck; others believe in magic. Most of us believe in love. Also, a majority of us believe in the future. Moreover, more than half of the world's population believe in the existence of a supreme being—God.

In fact, some people put their faith in multiple belief-systems. Why? Well, as created beings, we all need someone or thing to believe in. Buddha, Athena, Apollo, Horus, Krishna, Vishnu, Thor, and Odin, are just some of the gods or beings revered by adherents from ancient times to the present. Those who do not acknowledge a tangible deity may identify an ephemeral being, spirit, specter or creature to believe in and revere. Then there are those who embrace belief systems that involve ancestral or animistic entities, mythological fairies and genies. This seems to suggest that when the Creator God is taken out of the picture, mankind tends to find someone or something else to believe in.

Some people believe in their favorite athletes or sports heroes. Others put their faith in business tycoons, industrialists, investment gurus, politicians, and social trendsetters. Sadly, the most disturbing truth is that too few people actually believe in themselves. Having lost faith in their own abilities or potential to achieve, they live their lives vicariously through the people they admire. Such self-doubt often manifests itself in a fixation with celebrities, movie and TV stars, politicians and sports heroes. Why is that?

Self-discounting Syndrome

In my view, some of the most celebrity-obsessed fans are probably suffering from what I call 'self-discounting syndrome.' That is, they have a bad habit of underestimating their true worth. They often talk about what they cannot do, rather than what they can. They complain about what they lack, while undervaluing the things they have. Too often, they view themselves as inept rather than competent. With such dim view of themselves, it seems easier to see admirable qualities like diligence, entrepreneurial spirit, heroism, and perseverance (noble virtues) in others rather than themselves. This means, their fixation with celebrity is in part, a tacit denial of their own self-worth.

Consider this!

Generally, self-doubt leads to defeat and failures. However, believing in oneself leads to self-confidence, which increases the prospect for achievements, progress and prosperity. Are you harboring a negative appraisal of yourself? Do you discourage yourself with negative self-talk? Are your own thoughts making you feel helpless, hopeless and worthless? If so, then it's time to start speaking positively to yourself. Even now, God wants to endow you with the inner faith to believe in yourself, believe in your abilities; believe in your dreams, believe in His divine plan and purpose for your life.

Buddha, the enlightened Guru said, "He is able who thinks he is able." That means what you think of your capability or potential for success can help to determine the prospect for a chosen pursuit. Indeed, you have the capability and the capacity to do good work and achieve meaningful goals. Knowing that, you must believe in yourself, have confidence in your aptitude and capacity to do good work; to live a life of promise and purpose.

You can do this by acting on the conviction that deep inside you lies the ability and mental faculty to realize your dreams. Indeed, every person possesses the wherewithal to succeed. Hence, it is needful to acknowledge the fact that God has equipped you with the will and skill to accomplish great things. Deep inside you lies the determination and passion to turn your ambitions into accomplishments. Most importantly, with divine assistance, even faint hope can materialize into actual attainment.

A New Pep-talk

Naturally, in order to obtain any meaningful goal, it is necessary to change your thinking about yourself. You can do this by giving yourself a new pep-talk. "I can do it! I can make my dreams come true. I can achieve my goals. I can learn a difficult subject. I can master a complex skill. I can become a great achiever."

Dear reader, almost everyone has moments of doubt, despair, and skepticism. Still, you need not feel downhearted because of self-doubt. Instead, you can bolster your confidence with positive pep-talk. That is, start speaking positive truths to yourself. Use encouraging affirmations and statements to inspire confidence and self-assurance. Like a coach who gives an impassioned speech to players, arousing enthusiasm and optimism about the expected outcome of a game; make a habit of speaking empowering and uplifting words to yourself and those you care about. Cheering yourself up with confidence-boosting pep-talks is a critical step in the new valuation of yourself. As Jesus said to the man who acknowledged his bouts with doubt, "All things are possible to those who believe." (Mark 9:23)

So, if you really want to live the life of a believer, you can. Like the father seeking a miracle from Jesus, you too can say with heartfelt sincerity, "Lord, I do believe; help me overcome my unbelief." (Mark 9:24).

<u>You can if you think so</u>!

In his letter of encouragement to the Philippians, the Apostle Paul wrote: "I can do everything through Christ who gives me strength." <u>(Phil. 4:13)</u> Like Paul, we may feel physically weakened by the harsh realities of life. But in Christ, we can find the strength to do what needs to be done. Our demanding schedule may cause us to experience fatigue. But in Christ, we can find the determination and empowerment to endure.

Dear reader, God has blessed you with the will and skill to succeed. Heaven has bestowed upon you the capacity and capability to accomplish your goals and realize your dreams.

And God's sustaining grace, strength, and wisdom is yours for the asking—especially when your life is guided by his will, plan and purpose. As the Scripture affirms, "Humanly speaking, it is impossible. But with God, everything is possible." <u>(Matt. 19:26)</u>

<u>Christ is a confidence builder</u>

Sometimes, you may feel overwhelmed, but in Christ, you can find the mental muscle to surmount every obstacle. Your life's experience may leave you feeling distressed and disappointed. But in Christ, you can find the courage to continue, endure hardships, deal with difficulties, and face daily challenges with conviction, grace and self-assurance.

Sadly, sometimes, we don't feel like our usual selves. Far too often, we tend to harbor negative views about our potential to achieve and succeed. Such a mindset makes it easy to think less of ourselves, and undervalue our self-worth. However, during those times, what we need most are new reasons to believe in ourselves again. Know this! Christ is a confidence builder. He can instill in you the assurance to believe in yourself, to act on your belief, dispel self-doubt with resolute determination and passion.

Product of God's Creative Genius

Even now, God wants you to remember, you are the product of his creative genius. You are precious in his sight. You are the apple of his eye. You are his prized possessions. You are his masterpiece, crafted by the master craftsman.

That means, you are peculiar, not commonplace. You are worthwhile, not worthless. You are exceptional, not ordinary. You come from premium stock, not common stuff. You are superior, not inferior. Once you begin to believe this, you have good reasons to act and feel like nobility instead of commoners. Indeed, your new self-appraisal would impel you to start acting like royalty instead of peasantry.

The Apostle Paul says it best. "But as many as received him, to them gave he power to become the sons of God, even to them that believe on his name" (John 1:12). As children of God, we are heirs of salvation and joint heirs with Christ. This makes us full-fledged members of God's family. We are endowed with the wherewithal to be all we can be, even if we never join the US Army.

Power in Positive Self-talk

Dear reader! God wants you to realize the power of positive self-talk. So the next time the devil afflicts you with self-doubt, tell yourself, "I may not know all the details now, and I may not even know how; but God's potential for my life is on the verge of fulfillment."

God will imbue you with the insight to acknowledge, "I'm more knowledgeable than I realize. I am smarter than I think. I am wiser than I seem. I am stronger than I imagine." (*A paraphrase of Christopher Robin's advice to Winnie the Pooh.*)

Conclusion

If you are afflicted with pessimism, ask God to imbue you with heavenly-inspired optimism. Then, with godly faith, you can feel capable and competent. With divine enablement, you can believe in yourself, and act on the plan to achieve your full potential. So start telling yourself, "With Christ, I can dream it; with his courage, I can achieve it. With my newfound faith, I can be confident in His strength."

The next time you find yourself feeling destitute, and despondent, helpless and hopeless, , you, like David, can say with confidence: "My help comes from the Lord" (Psalms 121:2). With this assurance, you too can be just as optimistic even in the worst circumstances.

The Last Word!

"I can do all things through Christ who strengthens me!" (Phil. 4:13).

Let us pray.

Heavenly Father, thank you for your words of encouragement today; for the reminder that self-doubt leads to defeat and failures. But believing in ourselves leads to achievements, progress and prosperity.

Endow us with the inner faith to believe in our abilities, believe in our dreams, and believe in your divine plan and purpose for our lives. May your Holy Spirit govern our actions, affect our attitudes, inspire our thoughts, and the decisions that we make each day. We ask these favors in Jesus name, amen.

Blessed

Introduction

<u>Opening Questions</u>

Do you know what it means to be blessed? Do you feel blessed right now? If not, would you like to be blessed? How does one become blessed?

<u>Religious Mindset</u>

The word blessed is most often heard among religious people. When something good happens to a religious person, one common expression is often heard—"the Lord has blessed me today." One familiar response to a kind deed goes like this. "Your kindness is a special blessing," or "Your gift/help was a blessing to me." When expressing feelings of appreciation to a friend, the following statement is often used. "It's a blessing to have a friend like you."

<u>Secular Mindset</u>

Likewise, secular people use the word lucky to convey similar ideas about their circumstance. When life is good, one might say, "I feel so lucky." When something favorable happens, it is often said, "I'm having a lucky day.' When things are going according to plan, the following expressions are often heard. "I'm having a lucky break;" or "Lady Luck is smiling on me."

Most often, the words blessed and lucky are used to express similar sentiments by both religious and secular people. To a godly person, being blessed means favored by God; to feel fortunate, receive divine grace or desirable gifts. Being lucky to an unbeliever means to have a favorable circumstance, lucky chance or a golden opportunity.

Defining Blessed

Generally, the word blessed is defined as being divinely favored, feeling fortunate; having a commendable circumstance—to feel contented or happy. Alternatively, being lucky means to have an auspicious or favorable chance, an unexpected, yet pleasing outcome. Synonyms of blessed are *blissful, contented, favored, fortunate, gladness* or *happiness*; *divinely anointed, consecrated*, etc. Word usage: *blessed* is an adjective, *blessedness* is a noun, and *blessedly* is an adverb. (http://dictionary.com)

User's Perspective

Oftentimes, the only difference between blessed and lucky depends on the user's perspective. To the spiritual person, all of life's events are controlled or directed by God. When the situation is good or pleasant, God's blessing is credited. When one is faced with troubles and trials, it is believed that God, in his wisdom, is shaping his/her character through hardships and struggles.

Such a belief is based on Rom. 8:28. "And we know that in all things, God works for the good of those who love him, to those who have been called according to his purpose."

Chance or Fate

However to the secular person, life's harsh realities depend on chance, fate, purposeful planning, impeccable timing, skill and ingenuity. Whenever something good happens, it is often credited to "a lucky break," or "a stroke of good luck." Whenever something bad happens, it is attributed to misfortunes or mishaps, "a stroke of bad luck or/bad karma." Knowing this, the following thoughts on blessing are worth pondering.

Quotable Quotes

Blessed are they who see beautiful things in humble places where other people see nothing" —Camille Pissarro. "Blessed are those who give without remembering, and take without forgetting"—Elizabeth Bibesco. "Blessed is he who has found his work; let him ask no other blessedness"—Thomas Carlyle.

"A contented mind is the greatest blessing a man can enjoy in this world"—Joseph Addison. "To be grateful is to find blessings in everything. This is the most powerful attitude to adopt, for there are blessings in everything"—Alan Cohen. "When I started counting my blessings, my whole life turned around— Willie Nelson.

A Biblical Viewpoint

The Bible teaches us that both chance and time is directed by God. Our origin has its beginning with God, and our ending is directed by Him. God is the author and finisher of our faith. So every event in our lives is the product of divine providence.

Starting in Genesis, the Great Creator called the earth, planets, stars, and all creatures into existence. However, when it was time to make man, God's creative voice was paired with His specialized attention to the crowning act of creation.

> And God said, Let us make man in our image, after our likeness: and let them have dominion over the fish of the sea, and over the fowl of the air, and over the cattle, and over all the earth, and over every creeping thing that creeps upon the earth. 27So God created man in his own image, in the image of God created he him; male and female created he them"—(Genesis 1: 26:27).

God's favoritism for mankind is evident in His personal involvement with the intricacies of our design.

> 7And the LORD God formed man of the dust of the ground, and breathed into his nostrils the breath of life; and man became a living soul"—(Genesis 2: 7).

The above texts evoke the imagery of a divine sculptor or potter, kneeling down, taking clay in His hands, and sculpting it into a mirror-image of himself. Then, stooping down even further, with intimate care, put his mouth upon that clay figure, and breathed life-giving breath into His earthen likeness. Quickened by energizing respiration, man became a living, talking, thinking soul.

Divinely Favored

This clearly shows that from the beginning, mankind was especially favored by God. The first man was singled out for personalized attention and affection. The soil that made him was extracted by the Creator, molded and shaped in the image of the Almighty. Then, Adam was brought to life by divine fusion, when living breath commingled with noble virtues, which flowed from the Blessed Lips into the blessed being. This was our first blessing.

Countering Sin's Curse

Sadly, sin was the curse God tried to shield us from. With the disobedience of Adam and Eve, blessing and curse became part of our new reality. However, despite the curse of sin, God has never stopped blessing us. Even today, God is eager to bless us, and make extraordinary efforts to negate the curse of sin.

The Psalmist shares a unique perspective on this topic. "Blessed is he whose transgressions are forgiven, whose sins are covered." (Psalm 32:1) This means, every time we are forgiven, we are blessed. And when we forgive others, we engage in a blessed exchange. Speaking through the prophet Jeremiah, God assures us with the following affirmation. "Blessed is the man who trusts in the Lord; whose confidence is in him." (Jer. 17:7)

Consider This!

Despite the curse of sin in our lives, it is still God's desire to bless us today. Why? That's because only His continuous blessings can counter sin's curse. Even now, God is ready to bless us today, much more than He did yesterday.

The question is: do you want to receive God's blessings? Then take the words of Jesus as confirmation of His blessed intentions towards us. Are you poor? "Blessed are the poor in Spirit, for theirs is the kingdom of God. Are you meek? "Blessed are the meek, for they shall inherit the earth." Are you merciful? "Blessed are the merciful, for they shall be shown mercy." Are you a peacemaker? "Blessed are the peacemakers, for they shall be called children of God." (Matt. 5:3-12)

Special Favors

The Holy Scripture affirms that believers are especially blessed when they meet certain conditions. Knowing this, the Psalmist proclamation seems fitting here. "O Lord of

53

hosts, Blessed is the man who trusts in you!"—(Psalms 48:12)

In another instance, David said: "Blessed are they whose ways are blameless, who walk according to the law of the LORD—(Psalm 119:1). On one occasion, Jesus explains to Thomas the blessed benefit of believing in him, even without His physical presence. "You believe because you have seen me. Blessed are those who believe without seeing me"—(John 20:29). In responding to the kind words of a certain woman, Jesus said: "Yea rather, blessed are they that hear the word of God, and keep it"—(Luke 11:28).

Though divine grace, forgiveness and loving-kindness are available to everyone, it is God's good pleasure to bestow special blessings on those who respond favorably to His entreaties. He is also eager to bless us beyond measure for the things we do to please Him. Like a parent who gives special favors to a dutiful child, God is especially generous to those who practice godliness, live righteously, and serve others cheerfully.

Conclusion

From the beginning, it was God who blessed us, but the devil who cursed us. Even today, Satan stands ready to afflict us with disfavor. Thankfully, God is eager to bestow on us his divine favors. The evil one wants to destroy us, but God wants to save us. The devil actively seeks to oppress us, but God longs to redeem us, rescue us, and restore our divine status.

Dear reader, God has only good things in-store for us. And if we learn to obey Him, trust in Him, and put our lives in His hands, He will bless us abundantly. Through Christ's sacrificial death and resurrection, the curse of sin is already neutralized; and divine favors are ready to be poured out upon everyone who believes in the promises of His word.

The Last Word!

"Praise be to the God and father of our Lord
Jesus Christ, who has blessed us in the heavenly
realms, with every spiritual blessing in Christ."
(Eph. 1:3)—NIV

Let us pray.

Heavenly Father! Thank you for the blessings of your words; and all the special favors you show us. Lord, we long to receive more of your blessings each and every day.

Teach us how to develop a trusting relationship with you. And make us worthy to receive your grace, your divine gifts, loving-kindness, tender mercies, and the blessings of salvation. We ask these favors in Jesus name, amen.

Confidence

Introduction

<u>Opening Questions</u>

Are you a confident person? Do you feel confident about yourself, your ability to complete an important task, and obtain satisfactory results? Would you like to feel more confident about yourself? In this presentation, we will discuss the important role confidence plays in our lives.

The word confidence is often used to express feelings of certainty, strong belief in someone or thing. Being confident means to have faith in yourself; believe that you are able to achieve an important goal or realize your dream. This means, feelings of certainty about your ability to learn an important subject or master a critical skill is a sign of self-confidence.

<u>Feeling Competent and Self-assured</u>

Confidence is an important quality that makes us feel capable, competent and self-assured. Belief is the soil in which confidence grows. We can only feel confident about what we believe in. Confidence stems from a strong sense of certainty that we are able to do an important task well, achieve a worthwhile goal, and obtain desirable results from our efforts.

Defining Confidence

Naturally, the focus of this discourse compels me to submit a working definition of the keyword—confidence. Confidence is a firm belief in oneself or ability to do something worthwhile. Confidence is feeling self-assured or self-reliant, to trust fully in one's ability, fitness or readiness to do what is required. Additionally, having a firm belief in the pledge or promise of a trustworthy person is an expression of confidence. Synonyms of confidence are *certainty, assurance, faith or strong belief,* etc. Word Usage: *Confidence* is the noun, *confident* is the adjective, and *confidently* is an adverb. (http://dictionary.com) Knowing this, the following thoughts on confidence are worth pondering.

Quotable Quotes

"If my mind can conceive it, and my heart can believe it, I know I can achieve it"–Jesse Jackson. It's not who you think you are that's holding you back; it's who you think you're not–Denis Waitley. Marcus Garvey, who echoed the sentiments of Marcus Tullius Cicero, said: "If you have no confidence, you are twice defeated in the race of life. But with enough confidence, you have won even before you've begun"—Marcus Garvey, 1923.

The Confidence Factor

It is my belief that with enough confidence, an ordinary person can become an extraordinary individual. With enough confidence, a dunce can become learned, an amateurish person can become competent, and a coward can become courageous. Confidence makes a slow mind sharp, an average athlete a champion, and an untrained worker industrious and productive. Nothing boosts self-confidence more than doing what others said `could not be done.'

With confidence, you have what it takes to win when others fail, to persevere when others give up, to feel competent even when others perceive you as inept. Confidence empowers you to set achievable goals, and enables you to pursue them with determination and passion. Confidence equips you with the will and skill to aspire, to reach your full potential, and live the life God has in store for you.

Do you want to be more confident? Then know this! Despite challenges and harsh realities, you possess the mental and physical capacity to succeed, to triumph, and win. Confidence is the conviction that empowers you to identify achievable goals, and earnestly endeavor to pursue them. Confidence infuses you with the conviction that you are able to do your best work, and obtain a desirable outcome.

Clearly, confidence is an essential quality that enhances

your ability to achieve, to excel, and do amazing things. Reality teaches us that people who feel confident in themselves are more likely to obtain their goals and realize their dreams. Conversely, those who lack confidence tend to fail more often; and are more prone to give up on themselves, abandon their goals, and simply stop trying.

Dear reader, it is God's desire to infuse you with the confidence you need to obtain desirable results from your efforts. God knows that lack of confidence leads to discouragement and despondency. All of heaven is genuinely engaged in helping us live courageously, work productively, and think progressively. With that in mind, let's consider the divine admonition in the passage below.

> "Do not throw away your confidence; it
> will be richly rewarded. You need to
> persevere; so that when you have done
> the will of God, you will receive what
> he has promised." (Heb. 10:35-36)

Endeavor to Endure

In case you are unsure about what the writer is trying to convey, let me explain. He is saying, "Do not abandon your dreams; do not give up on yourself. More importantly, resist the urge to quit because of difficulties, hardship or obstacles. Instead, endeavor to endure, persevere, and keep on striving until you reach your goals."

<u>You are what you think</u>!

Sadly, many people lack the confidence they need to succeed. Too often, they allow disbelief and self-doubt to keep them from doing their best. Instead of believing that they are able, they tell themselves they are unable. But in the words of <u>Buddha</u>, the Enlightened Guru, "He is able who thinks he is able."

That means, if you think like a winner, you can win. If you think like a champion, you can triumph. If you believe in your ability to achieve, you can become an exemplary achiever. If you act boldly, plan confidently, and work courageously, you can accomplish great things, and live an amazing life.

<u>Pray Earnestly and Persistently</u>!

The next time you feel less than capable, call upon God in faith; pray earnestly and persistently for divine help. The Apostle John shares the following viewpoint on this matter in the text below.

"This is the confidence we have in approaching God. If we ask anything according to his will, he hears us. And if we know that he hears us—whatever we ask—we know our request will be granted." (<u>1 John 5:14-15</u>)

Conclusion

God knows that confidence is an empowering force. Confidence takes the place of weakness, and replaces it with strength. Confidence takes the place of pessimism and replaces it with optimism. Confidence takes the place of hopelessness and replaces it with hopefulness. Confidence boosts the can-do attitude; bolsters the belief that your goals are achievable, and your dreams are realizable. Confidence helps you to realize, "you can do it," you can make it happen; you can deal with difficulties and handle life's challenges effectively.

Knowing this, the following questions are worth asking. Is there a goal you would like to accomplish? Is there a dream you would like to pursue? Would you like to live a successful life? Are you ready to plan confidently, work courageously, and project the image of a competent and capable person? Then ask God to boost your level of confidence. He will enable you to believe in yourself, believe in your dreams, and believe in divine providence that wills your success.

The Last Word!

> "Do not throw away your confidence; it will be richly rewarded. You need to persevere, so that when you have done the will of God, you will receive what he has promised." (Heb. 10:35-36)

61

<u>Let us pray</u>!

Heavenly father! Thank you for the confidence-boosting word of encouragement. Lord, I want to feel more confident about myself, my ability to achieve my goals and realize my dreams.

Give me the faith to believe that with your help, I am capable; in your strength, I am strong. With your support, I am confident and competent. Embolden me with faith and fortitude to act boldly, live courageously, and plan with expectancy of a promising future. Endow me with confidence-boosting faith to believe in myself; and the conviction that I too can accomplish great things, and live a fulfilling life. Instill within in me the earnest endeavor to do all that you require.

Bestow upon me your divine enablement to be dutiful in my work, earnest in my efforts, and steadfast in my pursuit of excellence. Bless my efforts and endeavors; empower me to aim high, and claim the promises of Scripture. May your Holy Spirit guide my actions and decision-making. Favor me with your divine grace. That way, my achievements will bring glory and honor to your holy name. I ask these favors in Jesus name, amen.

Contentment

Introduction

<u>Opening Questions</u>

Are you a contented person? Do you feel content with your life nowadays? Do you know what it means to be content? Would you like to experience true contentment?

Some people spend a lifetime seeking contentment, but seldom experience it. Others seem to experience it on occasion, but their state of contentment is fleeting; lasting only a short while. Then there are those who seem perpetually content, it is easy to feel envious of them.

<u>Contentment: a State of Mind</u>

Sadly, the word contentment is so easily misunderstood, many people think of it as a wish or an ideal to strive for. They often surmise that when Lady Luck smiles upon them, they will experience contentment. But until then, they'll just wait their turn expectantly.

Ironically, contentment is not a goal to be obtained, not an ambition to be pursued, nor an ideal to work towards. Instead, it is a state of mind, an emotional or mental acceptance of one's status, despite discomforts or inconveniences. Contentment is a cheerful mindset that enables us to cope with life's harsh realities.

Defining Contentment

Generally, contentment means being at ease, feeling satisfied with one's circumstance; having a comfortable, happy state of mind, a cheerful and pleasant mood. It is a fulfilling feeling, a calming and peaceful disposition. Synonyms of contentment are enjoyment, fulfillment, happiness, satisfaction, and serenity. *Contentment* is a noun, *content* is an adjective, and *contently/contentedly* are both adverbs. http://dictionary.com

Most often, our dreams are shaped by our desires. Our Ambitions are driven by an innate longing for achievement, attainment and recognition, an intense drive to obtain desirable status and success. However, happiness depends not on the abundance of material possessions, but on our willingness to enjoy what we already have. Contentment is the result of a conscious choice to find satisfaction in less than ideal circumstances. Knowing this, the following thoughts on contentment are worth pondering.

Quotable Quotes

"Contentment is natural wealth; luxury is artificial poverty"—Socrates. "Health is the greatest possession. Contentment is the greatest treasure. Confidence is the greatest friend— Lao Tzu." "Contentment is the pearl of great price; and whoever obtains it at the expense of a thousand desires makes a wise and happy purchase— John Balguy."

One Unknown Poet puts this way. "As a rule, man's a fool. When it's hot, he wants it cool. And when it's cool, he wants it hot. Always wanting what is not." Buddha shares a very insightful sentiment that seems fitting here. "Health is the greatest gift. Contentment is the greatest wealth, faithfulness the best relationship."

Being Content

Surprisingly, contentment does not depend on good fortune. Contentment does not require notoriety (fame), prosperity or wealth. One does not need luxury or material possessions to be content. Instead, it only requires one thing—the decision to make oneself content in good times and bad, with luxury or poverty, prosperity or adversity.

Addictive Pastime

In our consumer-driven culture, shopping has become an addictive pastime. Why? Well, for one thing, advertisers and marketing experts have turned the art of selling into an indulgence industry. Consequently, some of us are easily enticed to go shopping when we don't need to, spend money we don't have, and buy stuff we can't afford. Even more worrisome is the fact that far too many shoppers tend to spend their hard earned income acquiring stuff they can do without. Often, such unnecessary purchases are done to "impress folks who care little about them."

Sadly, one of the ill-effects of sin is the craving for things we do not need. Too often, we hanker for what we cannot have, and pine over what we lack. Hence, our preoccupation with getting more stuff prevents us from appreciating the things we already have. Thus, the desire to acquire more material possessions robs us of the simple pleasures that come from enjoying the things we own. Amidst their closets-full of clothes, and rooms decked with high-end figurines, furnishings, and other prized possessions, some are still haunted by discontentment.

Discontented in Paradise

This was the cause of Adam and Eve's disobedience. Though they lived in the garden of God, the first couple felt their creator was depriving them of something desirable. Though she had everything she needed to be happy, Eve became discontented with God, mostly because of one forbidden fruit. The Garden of God was surrounded by an ecological nursery and decorative green-space. Even so, Eve was apparently discontented because of a lone prohibition against eating one fruit.

Consider this!

Her home was earth's first botanical garden; yet she was dissatisfied with her life. What was the end result of her dissatisfaction? In exchange for a mouthful of fruit, she traded paradise for the chance to know both good and evil. Under the beguiling power of the serpent, she was

66

convinced that the knowledge of good and evil was something to be desired. Alas, the consequence of her bad decision is a polluted, problem-plagued, and sin-sick world. Nevertheless, God had a different plan for the human family. From the beginning, it was God's desire to teach us the secret of contentment.

Finding Contentment

Ideally, the first step towards finding contentment is learning to differentiate between our needs and wants. We need food, protective and warm clothing, shelter, and a safe environment in which to live, learn, work and worship. Most people in developed countries have all these things. Yet, far too many are as discontented as Eve was in Paradise.

Some people spend much of their time, efforts and energies trying to acquire more things to satisfy their desires, they seldom get to enjoy what they already have. Far too many people spend their days and nights working extra hours, earning more money in order to buy the latest gadgets, high-priced automobiles, and other status symbols. Ironically, they scarcely take the opportunity to appreciate those items once they buy them. That's because shortly after their latest purchase, new models with advanced features are being advertised.

Some homeowners have so much stuff, they store them in the garage, and park their cars outside. Those without garages store their extra stuff in commercial storage facilities. Once they realize many of those things are seldom used, they have a garage sale. After selling some of the things that clutter their living spaces, they must summon extraordinary will-power to avoid starting the process all over again.

Knowing this, manufacturers normally make the newest models of gadgets, devices and gizmos look more enticing than the previous versions. Consequently, some consumers rarely get much enjoyment from their latest purchases. Why? Partly because the coolest, ingenious functions seem to be in the model that just hit the market. Our consumer-driven culture makes it easy to believe the commercials that tell us the things on sale are the items we "must have" to be content. Lacking the ability to differentiate between needs and wants, it's hard to resist the temptation to buy more stuff.

Even more distressing is the fact that getting more stuff diminishes their capacity to cherish the things they have already. Why is that? Probably because they mistakenly believe that they need more things to be happy. Most people living in developed countries can easily obtain essential supplies to meet their daily nutritional needs, and indulge in desirable creature comforts, at least, on a semi-regular basis.

Additionally, some find it hard to constrain their innate craving for gourmet provisions, designer garments and accessories, luxurious and opulent dwellings, while taming their desire to hobnob with aristocrats and celebrities. The truth is, overcoming the obsession to acquire more stuff will enable us to realize that some of life's most treasured moments come from the enjoyment of simple pleasures.

The second step in finding contentment is to value relationships more than things. True contentment has little to do with how much stuff we have. Instead, it depends mostly on our ability to tame our desires and learn to enjoy life's precious moments. It also entails strengthening our relationship with our loved-ones, learning to value today's opportunities, while counting present blessings. Christ's cautionary note is worth repeating here. "…Watch out! Guard yourselves against every form of greed. For a man's life does not consist in the abundance of his possessions." (Luke 12:15)

One essential action-plan for finding contentment is to start with our daily decisions, hour by hour, and moment by moment. We must decide to be content with what we have, even if what we have is just adequate. We must also learn to make the best of our current circumstance, while seeking meaningful ways to experience emotional fulfillment, despite our immediate situation.

We can do this my making earnest efforts to become stronger, wiser, and more resilient amidst life's changing fortunes. By adopting this mindset, we put ourselves in the right frame of mind to appreciate life's little blessings.

Then, when God bestows upon us substantial favors, we will be ready to appreciate them with an attitude of gratitude. Such gratitude will enable us to express our thankfulness for his loving-kindness and providential care towards us. The Apostle Paul explains the mindset of a contented believer in the following text.

> "I am not saying this because I am in need, for I have learned to be content whatever the circumstances. I know what it is to be in need, and I know what it is to have plenty. I have learned the secret of being content in any and every situation, whether well fed or hungry, whether living in plenty or in want. I can do everything through him who gives me strength. (Phil. 4:11-13)

Conclusion

Dear Reader, it is God's intent to fill our lives with contentment. However, our sinful nature prevents us from experiencing true satisfaction. Though everyone wants to find contentment in life, most people don't know how to obtain it.

Would you like to know the secret of contentment? Then take to heart Paul's advice to Timothy! "A godly life brings huge profits to people who are content with what they have. (1st Tim. 6:6)

70

Surprisingly, contentment is not dependent on the value of our personal possessions. Happiness is not contingent on an ideal circumstance or perfect environment. Contentment is not something that magically happens to us when everything is just right. Instead, it is the result of a deliberate effort to be content, no matter what. True contentment springs from the desire to please God, to trust Him with our future and destiny; and allow Him to fulfill His divine purpose in our lives.

The Last Word!

"Keep your lives free from the love of money and be content with what you have, because God has said, 'Never will I leave you; never will I forsake you.'" (Heb. 13:5)

Let us pray.

Heavenly father, Thank you for your encouraging words. We are grateful for the reminder that ensuring our contentment is your good pleasure. Lord, we long to experience true contentment in our lives. Like the Apostle Paul, enable us to experience contentment in good times and bad, in sickness and in health, in luxury and poverty, prosperity and adversity.

Teach us how to live godly lives, and enable us to learn the secret of contentment. Lord, Infuse us with an attitude of gratitude. This way, we too can experience fuller, richer and more satisfying lives. We ask these favors in Jesus name, amen.

Dreams

Introduction

<u>Opening Questions</u>

Can you remember your childhood dreams? Have you achieved any of them? Do you still believe in them? Do you have the same dreams you had as a child? Are you currently engaged in the pursuit of any dream? If not, why not?

<u>Dream-dalliers</u>

Since there are many kinds of dreamers in life, I'll begin this discussion by describing a few of them. The first group I call 'dream-dalliers.' These people have dreams in their hearts, but they spend most of their days in hazy-dazy ways, without striving to fulfill any of them. Instead, they fritter their time away doing meaningless things and engaging in trivial pursuits.

<u>Dream Sloths</u>

The second group I call 'dream-sloths.' Like the sloths of the wild, their minds are abuzz with mental activities, and dream-related thoughts. But mentally or physically, they are mostly unaffected by their dreams. Due to prolonged lethargy, oversleep or habitual use of mind-altering substances, their muscles are flabby, lacking in strength, and their will-power deficient—devoid of passion. This makes them ill-equipped for even the most menial dream-pursuits.

Dream Stealers

The third group I call 'dream stealers.' Lacking the drive to pursue their own dreams, they've abandoned them. Having no meaningful pursuit to occupy themselves with, they turn their attention to anyone who seems driven by a dream. Dream stealers tend to see the pitfalls and risks involved in any endeavors for dream fulfillment. Sadly, they seldom see the opportunities or possibilities for realizing their own dreams.

Dream stealers love to share their dream-killing ideas with anyone who seems determined to pursue a desirable dream. They are also quick to tell others their dreams are either too big or too unrealistic. Seeing the years of their lives come and go without the fulfillment of any dream, they seem visibly bothered by those who are actively engaged in dream-pursuit.

What dream stealers fail to realize is that everyone needs a dream to work towards, including themselves. We all need something within us to spark the desire for achievement and meaningful success. Humans have an inborn fondness for dreaming and making earnest efforts to turn cherished dreams into reality.

Defining Dreams

Naturally, the focus of this discourse necessitates devising a working definition of dream. Dream: *an involuntary vision occurring to a person while awake.* Webster.com defines dream as a visionary creation of the imagination. Synonyms of dream are *aim, aspiration, desire, hope and objective.* Word usage: depending on the context, *dream* can be used as an adjective, noun or verb; *dream, dreamed, dreamt* and *dreaming* are verbs.

Most people know that the word dream can have multiple meanings. Knowing this, I'm not talking about the extra-sensory or visual sensations that accompany deep sleep. Furthermore, the aspect of dream in this discourse should not be confused with wishful thinking. Instead, the dream I'm describing is what gives birth to our innate impulse or inner drive to set meaningful goals and work towards achieving them.

Furtive soil of achievement

Deep within us is an aspirational desire, impelling and propelling us forward, prodding us towards purposeful dream-pursuit. Such burning desire can be easily synthesized into fertile soil from which our inmost yearnings spring forth. Dreams are the seeds that sprout into life, spurring creative ideas, and the entrepreneurial spirit. Dream fulfillment leads to inventions and innovations. Such dreams turn the mind into a productive workshop, where concepts are turned into designs; and sketches are transformed into useful items or products. Dreams are the wellsprings from which our creative effort and ingenious craftsmanship emerge. Knowing this, the following thoughts on dreams are worth pondering.

Quotable Quotes

"To accomplish great things, we must dream as well as act" —Anatole France. "Allow your dreams a place in your prayers and plans. God-given dreams can help you move into the future He is preparing for you"—Barbara Johnson. The invariable mark of a dream is to see it come true" — Ralph Wald Emerson.

"Dreams are like stars. You may never touch them; but if you follow them, they will lead you to your destiny"— Liam James. "Don't let anyone steal your dream. It's your dream, not theirs"—Dan Zadra. "Only as high as I reach, can I grow. Only as far as I seek, can I go. Only as deep as I look, can I see. Only as much as I dream, can I be" – Karan Ravn.

Dream Fulfillment

One benefit of striving to live our dreams is the experience of true happiness. Most people are especially happy when they achieve a noteworthy goal or realize an important dream. However, nothing breaks a man's spirit like a broken dream and shattered hopes. The wise man Solomon said it best. "Hope deferred makes the heart sick, but a dream fulfilled is a tree of life." (Prov. 13:12) New Living Translation

Driven by a Dream

Successful entrepreneurs, inventors, innovators and leaders of great enterprises are those who manage to turn their dreams into reality. Dream fulfillment requires a single-minded focus on goal achievement plans, success strategies, and strong determination to persevere, despite setbacks. Dreams empower the courageous and daring to risk failures, leap over hurdles, and surmount obstacles. Those driven by dreams tend to win when others lose. Like Elon Musk, Jeff Bezos, Steve Jobs, Bill Gates and Oprah Winfrey, such dreamers tend to become living examples of conquest and success.

Dreams and Dreamers

Ironically, every single person has a dream yet to be realized. Sadly, not everyone makes the necessary efforts to turn their dreams into reality. Some people dream dreams, but due to inaction, both the initial awareness and inner drive naturally wanes. Each year that comes and goes without any meaningful goal achievement makes it easier to forget their dreams altogether. Others just talk about their dreams, but make no plans, and develop no strategy for any serious dream pursuits.

A Dream Worth Pursuing

However, true dreamers are so inspired by their dreams, they are determined in their hearts to pursue them, no matter what. In time, they earn their place among the fortunate few who get to live their dreams. It is almost impossible to realize our dreams without first believing that we can. Why? That's because any dream worth having is worth pursuing!

You must be convinced that you have what it takes to make your dreams come true. One crucial factor in any goal-achievement plan is an unshakable belief in your physical capability and mental capacity for successful dream-pursuit. That is, you must believe in your dreams, believe in yourself, believe in your abilities to pursue and achieve them. Why? Well, for one thing, if you don't believe in your own dreams, why should anyone else? The truth is, you are the best salesman for your own ideas. You are the chief spokesperson to convince others about your prospect for dream-fulfillment! More importantly, having faith in your dreams will stir within you the self-confidence that drives successful dream pursuit.

Naturally, confidence forms the basis for your faith. Faith is an essential element in any important pursuit. Faith inspires conviction. Conviction compels you to take action. And your actions, when spurred by your dreams, help to produce the kind of results you anticipate.

<u>Consider This</u>!

It is most unfortunate that *Dream Dalliers, Dream Sloths* and *Dream Stealers* do not understand the true nature of a dream. What they fail to realize is that a man without a dream lacks the internal motivation that propels great achievers to think the unthinkable, attempt the improbable, and make the impossible realizable. Every would-be achiever should understand that a man without a dream is a man without a plan. A man without a plan is a man without a vision. A man without a vision is a man without hope. And a man without hope is a soul who lacks the wherewithal to cope with life's harsh realities.

<u>Dream-fulfillment Strategy</u>

So, how does one attain dream-fulfillment? Simple! First, learn how to recognize your own dream. Think about that unfulfilled desire, that un-relenting longing, that inner yearning you've been unable to contain. Ask a guidance counselor, mentor or a respectable person who is recognized for his/her good judgment, keen insight, and powers of discernment. Most importantly, ask God (if you are a believer) to help you distinguish dream from fantasy, and advise you on a practical action-plan to aid your dream pursuit.

Then, muster the courage to believe in yourself, and believe in your dreams. You must also believe that God has endowed you with the wherewithal to achieve the dream he has placed in your heart. With that in mind, take ownership of your dreams! Cherish your dreams! Treat your dream-pursuit like a personal quest. Pursue your dream with strong determination, a single-minded focus and passion.

You can start by taking steps to determine the most practical means and methods of pursuing your dream. Also, consider plans and strategies that will enhance your efforts in making your dream come true. Most importantly, do your utmost to turn your dreams into reality. You can do this by adopting the attitude of a true dream chaser. Employ all your creative abilities and explore every promising avenue to enhance the success of your dream-achievement plan. Then, pursue your dreams unreservedly and wholeheartedly. Moreover, seek divine aid in every phase of your dream pursuit.

> "Trust in the Lord with all your heart; do not depend on your own understanding. Seek his will in all you do, and he will show which path to take." (Prov. 3:5&6)

Again, Solomon's advice is a fitting counsel for every dream chaser. "Commit to the Lord whatever you do, and your plans will succeed." (Prov. 16:3)

Conclusion

Consider this! Every person is born with a God-given dream. Knowing this, I can say with confidence, the will and skill to succeed is already within you. When you were knitted together in your mother's womb, threads of innate dreams were intricately woven into the fabric of your being.

Likewise, your Creator has endowed you with the aptitude and mental faculty to pursue and realize your dreams. Heaven has bestowed upon you talents, skills and abilities to achieve your goals and turn your dreams into reality. Indeed, God's sustaining grace, strength and wisdom is yours for the asking. Even now, God wants you to experience the feelings that come with dream-fulfillment.

That means, when your life is guided by divine will, it is God's good pleasure to help you attain dream-fulfillment. The scripture affirms that, "With God, all things are possible." So dream great dreams. Embrace your dreams. Internalize your dreams, so the desire to pursue them will burn within you like an ever-glowing ember.

Furthermore, make every effort to turn your dreams into reality. You can do this by adopting Paul's life-affirming maxim. "I can do all things through Christ who gives me strength"—(Phil. 4:13).

Let us pray.

Heavenly Father, thank you for your uplifting words; for reminding us of the role dreams play in our lives. Lord, it is you who put dreams in our hearts. Give us the courage and faith to believe in our dreams; cherish them, and pursue them with strong determination and passion.

Empower us to do all we can to make our dreams come true. Let your Holy influence guide our actions, inspire our hearts, as we strive to live the dreams you have placed within us. We ask these favors in Jesus name, amen.

Faith

Introduction

<u>Opening Questions</u>

Are you a person of faith? Is faith an important principle to you? Is your belief-system shaped by your faith? Do you have faith? Do you know what it means to live by faith?

Faith is such a simple word. But it is full of meaning and significance. For many people, faith is a doctrine that guides their lives. For others, faith is a concept that only religious people find value in. Some people with a secular mindset may think that faith is a concept shaped by an illogical and irrational belief system.

<u>Different Understanding of Faith</u>

Due to the conflict between religionists and secularists, it is easy to think that there are only two kinds of people in the world—the "faith-oriented" and "faith-skeptics." However, notwithstanding the theological notion that all humanity can be divided into just two groups, with regards to faith, I have a contrarian proposition. That is, it is more reasonable to believe that most people have different understanding of faith. Also, we cannot ignore the fact that ideological terms like faith-oriented and faith-skeptic can be misused to regard those we agree with favorably, and those we disagree with unfavorably.

Amidst such competing viewpoints, a new perspective is worth considering. There are reasons to believe that every single person practices faith on a daily basis. Let me explain. The man who goes to the barber shop for a haircut and a shave puts a lot of faith in someone he only knows on a superficial level. How so? Well, for one thing, most men do not choose a friend who happens to be a barber. They choose a barber based on criteria other than friendship. Though cultivating a close friendship with a barber who cuts one's hair for months or years may be convenient or desirable, it is neither automatic nor inevitable. That's because friendship is not an essential critical element in the barber-client relationship.

Transactional Faith

Furthermore, the barber uses a very sharp razor to cut the hairs around clients' ears and necks. What if that barber is angry with his neighbor? And just when he picks up that knife to cut the hairs around the client's neck, a surge of malicious feelings towards his foe overtakes him? Imagine what could happen if the barber mistakenly thinks of the person in his chair as his adversary.

Thankfully, ninety-nine percent of the time, the barber does his duty faithfully, and the client feels satisfied with his shave, pays for the service, and may even give a tip. Clearly, this is a interaction where faith is at work. I call it transactional faith.

Expectant Faith

Another scenario worth considering is our relationship with doctors. Each time we visit the doctor's office, we put our health and physical wellbeing into his or her hands. When we receive the prescription for drugs or other remedies, customarily, we follow the doctor's instructions without question.

Most of us hardly ever think about the fact that so many things can go wrong in the doctor's office. For instance, just a mere misspelling of the medicine prescribed by the doctor can have deadly consequences. Also, the doctor can easily be confused with the similarity of patients' names, and gives a potent prescription to a patient with a mild case of the sniffles.

Yet, we presume that the doctor is a professional, and is responsible enough to implement reasonable measures to prevent the occurrence of such an error. This too is another situation in which we exercise a lot of faith without thinking about it. I call this "expectant faith."

Faith by Proxy

How often do you ride airplanes? Before boarding your last flight, did you go to the cockpit and ask the captain any of the following questions? "Excuse me Sir or Madam! Are you sleepy or well-rested? Are you feeling okay today? Did you have a liquid breakfast/lunch before getting onboard? Do you have enough experience to fly this jetliner safely? Are you sure?"

Well, most passengers, including myself, wouldn't think of doing such a thing. Although I've flown in small, medium-size and large passenger aircrafts, logging hundreds of thousands of miles across continents and oceans, I've never felt the urge to question the captain or pilot in such a manner. Still, those are legitimate questions. However, most air-travelers take for granted that the airline company does its utmost to ensure the safety of all passengers.

Knowing this, we board the aircraft, feeling confident that we will have a safe flight. This is a good example of faith by proxy. That is, our faith in the airline company is invariably transferred to the cockpit crew hired to fly the aircraft. The same is true for the railroad agency. We trust the railroad corporation to hire only responsible engineers to operate the trains.

As you can see, faith is not just a religious concept. Instead, it is a principle that affects almost every aspect of our lives. This suggests that virtually everyone has faith in someone or thing.

Defining Faith

Due to the focus of this discussion, the following definition will prove useful. Faith is the belief that something is real, true or trustworthy—deserving of trust.

Faith is demonstrated in the confidence we place in someone or thing to do what is expected, to perform as promised. However, unlike confidence, faith is not a feeling. Nor is it a fanciful fixation with the unknown. Faith is not an obsession with a mystical phenomenon. Instead, it is a sense of certainty that an expected outcome is forthcoming. Faith is a firm conviction that one's belief is legitimate, reasonable and valid. Knowing this, the following thoughts on faith are worth pondering.

Quotable Quotes

"Reason is our soul's left hand, faith her right"—John Donne. "Faith is reason grown courageous"—Sherwood Eddy. "Faith is spiritualized imagination"—Henry Ward Beecher. "Faith is daring the soul to go beyond what the eyes can see"—William Newton Clark. "They are the weakest, however strong, who have no faith in themselves or their own powers"—Christian Nestell Bovee. "Faith is putting all your eggs in God's basket; then counting your blessings before they hatch."—Ramona C. Carroll

No Faith, No Trust

The Bible tells us, "Without faith, it is impossible to please God." Also, reality teaches us that without faith, it is impossible to trust anyone. Faith is the foundation on which trust develops. It is the essential element that all trusting relationships entails. That means, faith is the prerequisite for trusting in others.

The writer of Hebrews explains it like this. "Faith is the confidence that what we hope for will actually happen; it gives us assurance about things we cannot see." (Heb. 11-1) New Living Translation)

Assumptive Faith

When my first son was a baby, I often picked him up, threw him into the air and caught him on his way down. He liked it so much he giggled with glee, hinting to me that I should do it again. Although he knew that falling was a possibility, still, he assumed that his dad would catch him before he fell to the ground. This is what I call assumptive faith. That is, he merely assumed that the second experience would turn out just like the first.

Aside from the fact that I caught him earlier, he had no assurance I would do it again. The truth is, I made no promise to catch him. Still, he had no reason to suspect that I might have allowed him to fall. Instead, he was convinced that he could count on me to catch him. Hence, he was exercising assumptive faith, long before he understood the concept.

Anyone can have faith

The above recollection proves that there are different kinds of faith. The faith practiced by religious people is just one form of faith. The truth is, anyone can have faith. And every person can have a faith-based experience with God.

Also, belief in the Judeo-Christian God is one of the dominant forms of godly faith.

Religious faith is based on one's belief in a deity, god, or supernatural being. Still, the Christian doctrine of faith is not just a religious concept. Instead, it is a belief-system based on the claims of Scripture and our experience with the divine. God does not expect us to exercise blind faith without any confirmation or proof that he is trustworthy—deserving of our trust.

Faith-based Relationship

Actually, the Bible encourages all believers to prove all things. Scripture encourages readers to take God at his word, believe in the certainty of his promises, and cultivate a faith-based relationship with him. When we put our trust in God, He inducts us into the society of faithful believers. Like Joseph, Esther, Job, and Daniel, God qualifies us as worthy recipients of His divine favors--heaven's best gifts, and sufficient grace. The Lord's command to his people in the text below helps to illustrate this point.

> "If you follow my decrees and are careful to obey my commands, I will send you rain in its season and the ground will yield its crops and the trees of the field their fruits." (Lev. 26:3-4)

Incentivized Faith

In the passage above, God gave the Israelites incentives to have faith in him. The incentives are promised blessings and divine provisions. God is not a frivolous or whimsical parent. He does not ask us to do anything just because...

Stalwarts of Faith

The writer of Hebrews extols the role of faith in the life of believers. He asserts, "By faith, Abel was declared righteous, and obtained the promise of eternity. By faith, Enoch escaped death, was taken into heaven, and is now enjoying the rewards of the faithful.

The scripture tells us, it was by faith, that Noah built a boat to save all those who wanted to escape the flood. Furthermore, it was by faith, that Abraham obeyed God, and embarked upon a spiritual sojourn with Him. With his eyes of faith, the faithful patriarch looked beyond the bounds of earth, and saw a celestial city, whose builder and maker is God." You can read more about this in Heb. 11.

The Scripture records numerous instances where believers' faith bolsters the foundation of religious belief. Indeed, faith forms the basis for godly living, the expectation of special blessings, divine favors, healing, and other spiritual rewards. In affirming the faith of the Woman with a bleeding disorder, Jesus declared: "Daughter, your faith has made you well. Go in peace! Your suffering is over."(Mark 5:34)

Living Faith

In reassuring Jairus concerning his dead daughter, Jesus said: "Don't be afraid! Just have faith." (Mark 5:36)

When awakened by the disciples who were fearful for their lives, Jesus, before rebuking the winds and waves, wondered out loud. "Why are you fearful? O ye of little faith!" (Matt. 8:26)

In granting Blind Bartimaeus' request, Jesus said to him: "Go, for your faith has healed you." Instantly, his vision was restored, enabling him to follow Jesus on his journey. (Mark 10:52)—New Living Translation.

Concerning the friends of a paralytic man who brought their buddy to the healing teacher, Jesus, "…seeing their faith, declared, son, be of good cheer; your sins are forgiven." (Matt. 9:2)

Hearing the Centurion's unusual recommendation, "Speak the word only, and my servant will be healed;" Jesus remarked: "I have not found so great faith, no, not in Israel." (Matt. 8:5-10)

In commending the persistence of a Phoenician woman, Jesus said: "Dear Woman, your faith is great! Your request is granted, according to your desire. And her daughter was healed that very hour." (Matt. 15:24-28)

Clearly, faith is an integral part of our religious beliefs. Most importantly, faith is an essential element in our relationship with God. Putting our faith into practice is never a fruitless exercise. Instead, it is a rewarding part of our religious experience.

Worthwhile Faith

Dear reader, God does not require blind faith without any assurance or evidence of his faithfulness. Instead, he rewards those who have faith in him, and judges those who doubt him. God is willing to prove himself deserving of our obedience, trust and worship. That's why he encourages us in this manner. "Prove all things; hold on to what is good." (1 Thess. 5:21)

Ironically, godly faith is not always contingent on physical evidence. Similarly, sincere faith doesn't always demand proof. Equally true is the fact that physical proof does not always affirm steadfast or unwavering faith. Instead, real faith naturally leads to trust. And trust is inextricably linked with a maturing and nurturing relationship with a trustworthy person.

Trusting Faith

Most of us are hesitant in putting our faith in a stranger.
Why? Well, for one thing, we don't know that person.
That's why he or she is called a stranger! But after getting
better acquainted, we are able to judge whether or not the
former stranger is someone we can put our faith in—a
person who is deserving of our trust.

Naturally, the more dependable or reliable someone
becomes, the easier it is to have faith in him or her. The
same is true with the Lord. That's why Jesus tells his
followers the following. "And whatever you ask in prayer,
you will receive, if you have faith. (Matt. 21:22)

Conclusion

Dear reader, Christ is calling us into a faith-based
relationship with him. He wants to reveal himself to us.
Through his words, he offers us a fuller knowledge of his
will and ways for our lives. He longs for us to have a
personable, faith-based experience with him.

Knowing this, it is hard to resist asking another important
question. How does one get faith? The Apostle Paul
informs us with the following text. "And faith comes from
hearing, and hearing by the word of Christ"— (Rom.
10:17)

Naturally, during the Greco-Roman Period when Paul lived, only the affluent and especially privileged people learned to read and write. Back then, the most common way people became literate was to be taught by a tutor, attend an elite school, or hire a capable teacher. Fortunately for us, most people today learn to read and write in public schools or other private institutions. Hence, we could easily paraphrase Paul's statement today in this way. `Faith comes by reading or learning about God; and God speaks to us in the pages of Scripture.

So take Peter's advice! Put your faith in the promises of scripture. Believe and obey God's word. Anchor your faith in the foundation of God's sacred truth. He will endow you with spiritual discernment and understanding of His redeeming love, tender mercies, and saving of Jesus Christ.

> "For this very reason, make every effort to add to your faith goodness; and to goodness, knowledge; and to knowledge, self-control; and to self-control, perseverance; and to perseverance, godliness; and to godliness, brotherly kindness; and to brotherly kindness, love. For if you possess these qualities in increasing measure, they will keep you from being ineffective and unproductive in your

knowledge of our Lord Jesus Christ."
(2 Pet. 1:5-8)

Faith-based Fellowship

Clearly, being a believer does not require us to practice blind faith in every aspect of our lives. Instead, Christ calls us into a faith-based relationship with Himself, the anointed envoy of the Father. Hence, those who put their trust in God will experience a loving and rewarding fellowship with him.

Now, the question is, what kind of faith do you have? What kind of faith do you want to develop? Are you ready to begin a faith-based fellowship with the Lord? Would you like to experience a loving, trusting relationship with Christ?

Then get to know God through his word. Build a friendship with him through daily devotion and prayer. Make a habit of exercising your new found faith. Seek new ways to put your faith into practice. Adopt godly faith as a new value-system for your life. The Apostle Paul said it best. "The righteous shall live by his faith." (Rom. 1:17)

The Last Word

Faith is the confidence that what we hope for will actually happen; it gives us assurance about things we cannot see. (Heb. 11:1)—New Living Translation

Let us pray.

Heavenly Father! Thank you for inviting us into a faith-based fellowship with you. Give us the courage to accept this invitation, so we can begin our journey of faith with you.

May your Holy Spirit work upon our hearts, minds and souls. Empower us and enable us to enter into a faith-based companionship with you. Lord, we long to experience a rewarding, saving, trusting relationship with our Faithful Father. Enjoin us into a fulfilling, nurturing, and faith-saving fellowship with you. Like Enoch, teach us how to live by faith, grow in faith, and walk in faith, from this earth into eternity. We ask these favors in Jesus name, amen.

Conquering your Fears

Introduction

<u>Opening Questions</u>

Are you a fearless or fearful person? Is there something you are afraid of? Are you easily frightened? What scares you the most? Almost every person is afraid of something. In fact, a lot of people are afraid to admit to their fears. Even more unsettling is the fact that some folks are afraid of things they haven't even encountered as yet.

Fear is a natural human reaction to danger–known or unknown. It is a common emotional response to unexpected, unfamiliar or surprising events. Most people are afraid of something, whether they want to admit it or not.

As children, some of us were afraid of the 'boogie man' or monsters. Others were afraid of scary animals, like dogs, mice and squirrels. As adults, some of us are afraid of bugs, lizards, and other kinds of creepy crawlies. For the purpose of this discussion, it is prudent to consult a standard dictionary for a working definition of the word fear.

Defining Fear

Most English dictionaries define <u>fear</u> as being afraid, a feeling of dread, fright or horror; being easily frightened, fearful or terrified. Synonyms of fear are agitation, angst, anxiety, faintheartedness, panic, etc. <u>Word usage</u>: *fear* can be used as a noun or verb; *fearless* and *fearful* are adjectives. *Fearfully* is an adverb.

<u>List of Fears</u>

Just a casual search on Google can generate various lists of top-ten fears. Going to the dentist is one such fear that causes many people to postpone doing dental work for as long as forever—longer, if possible. Fear of flying is one of the top-five fears for up to 20 million Americans. Many Internet websites lists 'fear of flying' among the fright-inducing activities for a lot of people. Also, fear of spiders and snakes trigger feelings of flight or fright in many women and girls—some wimpy men too.

Another fright-ridden activity is fear of public speaking. Surprisingly, some people are so afraid of making a presentation in public, given the choice between jumping out of an airplane (skydiving) and giving a speech in front of a live audience, they would prefer to jump from an airplane. What a frightening thought!

Some time ago, I shared this finding with a group of students. Being curious about the reason anyone would choose such an option, I asked my students directly about what they would likely do in a similar situation. Astoundingly, they too seemed inclined to jump with the parachuting group. Why? According to the most talkative member, "Though parachuting to the ground seems very scary, still, after jumping, it takes just a few minutes to land safely on the ground. However, giving a speech takes much longer. Also, at the end of the speech, some people tend to ask questions we are not sure how to answer. The anxiety that accompanies answering random questions only help to intensify the terrifying feeling that comes with giving a speech."

Naturally, my students' reluctance about speaking in front of an audience is understandable. After all, whenever I ask them to make presentations in class, they know I expect them to do it in a second language—English. This fact only helps to increase their anxiety. Still, there are those, whose aversion to public speaking makes the task equally fright-ridden, even when done in their native languages. Hence, given the chance, they would prefer to avoid it if possible.

Psycho-socio Fears

Obviously, everyone is afraid of something. Also, depending on our cultural, ethnic and socio-economic background, most of us are likely to experience certain kinds of fear at least once. For example, if you were born or raised in a developed country, or a major urban center, you are likely to be afraid of bugs, wasps, and other flying insects.

If you are uneducated, you are likely to be afraid of giving a speech, or doing a presentation in front of an audience. If you are a member of the lower class, you are likely to be afraid of flying. If you are Caucasian, you are likely to be afraid of minorities. If you are an ethnic minority, you are likely to be afraid of other minorities. If you are rich, you are likely to have a fear of becoming poor.

If you are poor, you are likely to dread the thought of friends or neighbors getting rich and leaving you behind. If you are an athlete, you are likely to have a fear of losing an important game, or getting a serious injury that could lead to permanent disability. If you are a professional person, you are likely to have a fear of failure. If you are a student, you are likely to have a fear of doing poorly on a major examination.

Fright-Ridden Anxiety

Naturally, fear is a real problem for anyone who is fainthearted or insecure. Also, when fear becomes chronic or crippling, it is referred to as a phobia—an extreme manifestation of fright-ridden anxiety. Most often, a distressing phobia can curtail our freedom, and rob us of our autonomy—limiting the quality of our lives in many ways.

Surprisingly, there are times when the feeling of fear is more frightening than the actual cause or source. Some people will dutifully follow meaningless routines because they are afraid of making changes. That's because making change involve the risk of uncertainties, which often trigger feelings of insecurities.

Fearful or Fearless

The truth is, no one is completely fearless. Everyone is fearful of something, some time. We all succumb to some kinds of fear on occasion. This seems to suggest that fear is a natural reaction to dangers, real or imagined. It is a normal response to life's unexpected events.

Most children are afraid of the dark. Some students are afraid of tests. Employees are afraid of losing their jobs. Business people are afraid of going bankrupt. Politicians are afraid of losing their next election. And nowadays, most of the western world is afraid of terrorism. In fact, since 9-11, one of my biggest fears is being an unlucky passenger on a hijacked jetliner.

Symptom of Insecurities

Ironically, some of us are afraid of the unknown. Some people are so terrified by fear, they are afraid of anything foreign, new or unfamiliar. Others are afraid of almost anything they don't understand. None of us are bastions of courage. We are all frightened by something at some point in our lives.

Sadly, fear is a natural consequence of sin. It is also a symptom of our insecurities. Since sin is the result of man's disobedience, fear is the manifestation of our inherent distrust and self-doubt. That is, when fear finds its way in our hearts, it causes us to feel freight-ridden, insecure and uncertain about our wellbeing.

Actually, it is the spirit of Satan that haunts, taunts, and tortures us with fear. Still, it was never God's intent that mankind would live in fear of anything. Instead, man was made to have dominion over every living creature; to rule over the whole world. This is evident in the command given to Adam and Eve.

> "And God said to them: 'be fruitful and multiply and fill the earth and subdue it and have dominion over the fish of the sea and over the birds of the air and over every living thing that moves on the earth." (Gen. 1:28)—ESV

Shortly after the flood, Noah and his family were commanded to repopulate the earth, and establish a new civilization. Even then, the command given in Eden was essentially the same.

1"And God blessed Noah and his sons, and said unto them, Be fruitful, and multiply, and fill the earth. **2**And the fear of you and the dread of you shall be upon every beast of the earth, and upon every fowl of the air, upon all that moves upon the earth, and upon all the fishes of the sea; into your hand are they delivered." (Gen. 9:1-2)— King James 2000

Fear: A Consequence of Sin

Starting in Eden, it was God's intent that all creatures would be afraid of us, not us afraid of them. Sadly, the Serpent enticed man to distrust his creator, and regard the 'knowledge of good and evil' as a virtue rather than a source of vice. The end-result of that distrust is death, disease and fear, etc. In His dealings with humanity, God has been earnest in his efforts to eradicate fear, and inspire us with bravery, courage, and holy boldness. Throughout the Scripture, God has always countered mortal fear in his people with heartening admonitions. "Do not be afraid!" "Do not lose courage!" "Fear Not!"

Fear in Joseph's Brothers

Fearing for their lives in Egypt, Joseph's brothers endeavored earnestly to pacify his steward. Their fearful demeanor prompted him to reply, "Peace be unto you, do not be afraid..." (Gen. 43:23)

Moses at the Red Sea

While trying to encourage the people to cease their murmuring, Moses admonished them, "Fear not! Stand still; and see the salvation of the LORD..." (Exod. 14:13)

Fear in Joshua

In bolstering Joshua's courage to bravely lead his people, God said: "This is my command—be strong and courageous! Do not be afraid or discouraged. For the LORD your God is with you wherever you go." (Josh. 1:9)

Combating Fear in Zechariah

In neutralizing the terror that gripped Zechariah, the angel said to him, "Do not be afraid, Zechariah; your prayer has been heard..." (Luke 1:11-12)

Combating Fear in Mary

In countering Mary's bout with fear at the sight of a divine being, Gabriel said, "Do not be afraid, Mary; you have found favor with God." (Luke 1:29-30)

So, when you are terrified, gripped with mortal fear, remember this, God stands ready to endow you with bravery, enliven you with courage, and infuse you with fearlessness. The Apostle Paul tells us: "For God has not given us a spirit of fear and timidity, but of power, love, and self-discipline." (2 Tim. 1:7)—NLT)

From the beginning, God wanted us to live daringly and courageously. Even now, God longs to neutralize our fears, and infuse us with bravery, boldness and stoutheartedness. God also knows that at the root of our fear lies distrust. And distrust, like a virus, is a mutated form of disbelief.

One of the dangers of disbelief is, it is the seedbed of doubt, in which cynicism and skepticism grows. When cynicism is nurtured by mistrust, it naturally develops into fear and dread, and finally, full blown hatred. Like his devilish onslaught on the Patriarch Job, Satan is prone to afflict the innocent; subjecting them to tragic misfortunes and ruinous loss. Without the assurance of godly faith, love, and divine providence, such agonizing adversity can cause grief-stricken people to blame God, rail against him, with cursing and swearing.

Consider Adam's response to God's call after eating the forbidden fruit. 10"And he said, I heard your voice in the garden, and I was afraid, because I was naked; and I hid myself." (Gen. 3:10) Notice also Cain's reaction towards God and his brother after his offering was rejected. 5"But unto Cain and to his offering he had not respect. And Cain was very angry, and his countenance fell." (Gen 4:5)

Actually, both Adam's and "Cain's reactions exemplify the manifestations of fear and dread run amuck. Although

105

Adam knew that it was impossible to hide from God, yet he tried to do it anyway. Being fully aware that there is no secret we can keep from God, Cain was hesitant in admitting to the heinous crime he had committed— fratricide. Realizing that his secret was known, Cain immediately felt a sense of dread about his guilt and resulting penalty. Terrified by the prospect of being held accountable by God, Cain declared, "My punishment is greater than I can bear"—(Genesis 4:13). When stricken with fear and dread, our capacity to reason can be easily short-circuited by emotional distress caused by life's harsh realities.

Consider this!

Fortunately, true love is the best remedy for emotional distress and distrust. Reality teaches us that it is hard to trust someone we do not love. This brings to mind the Apostle John's assertion. "Anyone who does not love does not know God, because God is love!" (1 John 4:8)

Another insightful comment shared by John seems fitting here. "There is no fear in love; but perfect love casts out fear; because fear involves punishment, and the one who fears is not perfected in love." (1 John 4:18)

Clearly, God's love is the only potent antidote for fear. And only divine love can eradicate all our fears. Thankfully, with God's everlasting love, we are equipped with the wherewithal to conquer our fears.

Conquering Our Fears

Now, the question is, how does one conquer fear? Simple!
Admit your fears to God. Tell him what you are afraid of.
Ask the Lord to bolster your courage, and help you face
your fears with spiritual stoutheartedness. Then, learn to
trust Him explicitly. Like the three Hebrew boys standing
before King Nebuchadnezzar, you can risk the royal rage of
an irate ruler by standing up for your convictions and
principles. Also, you can learn to depend on the Lord for
guidance, deliverance, and protection. That's because God
specializes in empowering us with bravery, boldness and
fearless courage.

Conclusion

Are you tired of being afraid? Then let God help you
overcome your fears. He wants to take your dread, and
turn it into daring. God longs to take your shyness and
inspire you with holy boldness. God wants to neutralize
your anxiety and imbue you with gallantry.

Whenever you feel overwhelmed with anxiety, let God take
your horror and turn it into heroism. Give God your
apprehension, and he'll replace it with conviction. Give
God your cowardice and he'll turn it into courage. Let go
of your timidity, and claim God's promises of love, power,
and the wherewithal to conquer your fears.

Infused with Holy Boldness

Dear reader, with God's enablement, you are more than brave. With his divine endowment you are more than conquerors. With your God-given empowerment, you are more than victorious. Like David, standing before Goliath, you are fearless! Like Daniel, daring to defy a king's decree, you are infused with holy boldness!

Like Paul, facing his execution, you can willingly surrender your life for the crown of glory. Like Jesus, who took the sting out of death, and loosen grave's grip on God's children, you are brave! You are daring! You are emboldened! You are triumphant! You are valiant! You can embrace this fearless disposition, not by might nor by power; but by the spirit of the living God.

The Last Word

> "The LORD himself goes before you and will be with you; he will never leave you nor forsake you. Do not be afraid; do not be discouraged."."
> (Deut. 31:8)

Let us pray.

Heavenly Father! Thank you for your inspiring words; for reminding us that fear is the byproduct of distrust. Lord, our sinful nature makes it is easy to distrust you sometimes.

Teach us how to love you as you love us. Put within our hearts your divine love, and make us perfect in your love.

Endow us with bravery, courage, and fearlessness. Enable us with divine empowerment to conquer our fears. Put within our hearts holy boldness to face our fears. Nurture the seeds of faith within us, and nourish them with your word.

Lord, we long to learn more about your will and purpose for our lives. May your divine grace eradicate our fears, and instill within us fearless fortitude and godly faith. We ask these favors in Jesus name, amen.

Remember...

Introduction

Opening Questions

Do you feel confident in your ability to remember things? Are you good at remembering dates, faces and names? Can you recite your favorite poem from memory? Can you sing your favorite song without a copy of the lyrics? How good is your memory these days?

Reliable Memory

Long ago, people were accustomed to memorizing important historical dates, events, names and places. They could also commit to memory epic poems, impressive speeches, and time-honored stories. Just a few decades ago, it was normal for students to recall fundamental principles of science and other important subjects from memory.

Unreliable Memory

Nowadays, most of us have a hard time relying on our memories to retain important information. Instead, we use notepads, daily planners, memos, Post-it notes, and personal digital assistance (PDA) to help us remember. With a variety of electronic data-storage and recording devices that store all sorts of information, many of us are using our memory a lot less.

When I was younger, I used to memorize the phone numbers of at least ten people. Why? That's because back then, I not only had to write those numbers down, I also had to dial each digit repeatedly whenever I needed to talk with one of my relatives or friends. The process of committing to memory those numbers involved physically writing them, and manually punching all those digits into the phone each time I called someone.

While using the rotary phone of that time, I had to stick my finger into a small slot, turn the rotor towards the right, all the way around, and let it go. I had to do this for all seven numbers. If the person lived out of town or in another zip code, then, I had to enter the area-code before each number. Whenever I made a mistake, I had to hang up, and repeat the process. Naturally, there were times when the line was busy. That meant, I had to hang up, wait a few minutes, and dial those numbers again. Such repetitive routines helped me memorized a long list of telephone numbers, addresses, and other important details.

Digital Memory Aids

Nowadays, thanks to technological advances, we can record up to a thousand numbers and other personal information, without ever committing any of them to memory. The last time I changed my phone service carrier, it took me more than a week to remember my current cell phone number. This proves that I am not immune to forgetfulness.

Each time I've moved from one location to another, I've had to forget my old address and phone numbers and memorize new ones in their places. Because of this, whenever someone asks me for my number, I sometimes hesitate in order to make sure I am giving the right one. In response to the strange look from the person asking, I usually offer the excuse: "I don't call myself."

Applicable Anecdote

One of the most unsettling results of forgetting is hurting my students' feelings by failing to connect the correct names with the right faces. Since some of their names are so similar, it's easy to mix up Jeong-min with Jong-min or Joong-min (males); Da-hee with Da-seul, Dae seom and Da-soo (females). Knowing this, I am often embarrassed whenever I meet a student and mistakenly call him or her the wrong name.

While teaching at a Sam Yook Language School in South Korea, I remember talking with a student after Vespers (Friday evening worship program). We were having a very pleasant conversation, when it occurred to me, I didn't know her name. So I decided to ask her, "What is your name?" When she told me, I responded: "Hmmm! Your

112

name sounds very familiar. Who is your teacher?" She said, "You are!"

Sadly, forgetfulness is one of the annoying reminders of our imperfection. It is also one of the unpleasant consequences of sin. Apparently, God must have known that we would be prone to forget. So he made a point of reminding us about what we should remember. The Bible records a few instances when God directly commanded his people to 'remember…!'

Remember!

"God said, Remember the Sabbath Day, and Keep it holy." (Ex. 20:8-11) Sadly, today, most people have apparently forgotten the only commandment God told us to remember.

Solomon tells us: "Remember your creator in the days of your youth; before the days of trouble come, and the years approach when you will say, I have no pleasure in them." (Ec. 12:1)

The prophet Isaiah records a monologue in which God earnestly entreated his people to recall events of the past. 9 Remember the former things of old: for I am God, and there is none else; I am God, and there is none like me— (Isaiah 46:9).

The writer of Hebrews admonishes us, "Remember those in prison as if you were their fellow prisoners, and those who are mistreated as if you yourselves were suffering. (Heb. 13:3)

While presenting another lesson about his coming kingdom, Jesus told his listeners, "Remember Lot's wife." The New Living Translation renders the following reading. "Remember what happened to Lot's wife." (Luke 17:32)

After reading this text, at least two crucial questions come to mind. One, "Who is Lot?" Two, "What happened to his wife?" Clearly, both are reasonable questions, each of which deserves a good answer.

A Little Known Person

Strangely enough, the Bible doesn't say much about Lot's wife. Instead, there are only two references to her in the whole Bible: one in each of the testaments—Old and New. Included in the narrative of Sodom and Gomorrah, Moses records the following. "But Lot's wife looked back, and she became a pillar of salt." (Gen. 19:26) Almost two thousand years later, Jesus used the story of Lot's wife as an object lesson with his listeners. "Remember Lot's wife!" (Luke 17:32)

Profile of Lot

While reflecting on this divine admonition, it is imperative that we answer the first question. "Who is Lot?" Lot was the nephew of Abram. When Abram left Haran, following God's command, "Lot went with him"—(Genesis 12:4).

After a while, Abram's and Lot's herdsmen started quarreling over pastureland. So Abram proposed that the two kinsmen separate to keep the peace between them. Since Abram's primary concern was to limit the possibility of a family squabble developing into a full-blown rift, he graciously allowed his younger nephew to choose the area he would settle in. The Scripture tells us, Lot chose the pastureland in the region where Sodom was located.

> 11Then Lot chose all the plain of Jordan; and Lot journeyed east: and they separated themselves the one from the other. 12Abram dwelled in the land of Canaan, and Lot dwelled in the cities of the plain, and pitched his tent toward Sodom—(Gen. 13:6-11).

Most likely, sometime after the separation, Lot met the woman who would become his wife while trading with the citizens of Sodom. His budding relationship with her could also help to explain why Lot eventually moved into the city of Sodom. Sadly, Lot seems like one of those men who followed his wife's lead, instead of him leading her and the family.

Profile of Lot's Wife

Now, unto the second question: "Who is **Lot's wife**?" If the claims of some Bible scholars are correct, Lot's wife was most certainly a citizen of Sodom. According to Gills Exposition of the Entire Bible, she was probably known as *Adith*. Other commentators identify her as *Irith*. Quite possibly, her father may have done some trade with Lot, and eventually introduced the Hebrew herdsman to his lovely daughter.

The Story Unfolds

In Gen. 19, we are told that two angels visited Lot's home in Sodom on the eve of its destruction. When the men of Sodom heard about the male visitors, they went to Lot's home, desiring to do abominable things to them. Lot tried to discourage their damnable intent. He even offered his two virgin daughters to them. Nevertheless, they persisted with their detestable demands.

Seeing this, the angels blinded their eyes, and instructed Lot to get his family members and loved-ones out of the city. Then the heavenly visitors gave them specific instructions about when to leave, and where to go. The couple was also told that Sodom would be destroyed because of the great wickedness there.

Stop Kidding Around!

Sadly, when Lot went to inform his sons-in-law about Sodom's impending doom, they thought he was just joking. So they stayed in Sodom. Early the next morning, the angels urged Lot and his family to flee the city at once. However, instead of making haste in heeding the angels' command, Mr. and Mrs. Lot began to linger forlornly. Seeing this, the angels grabbed them by the hand and led them out of the city.

Last Minute Bargain

Not wanting to go all the way to the mountains, Lot bargained with the angels to allow him to stay in the city of Zoar instead. The angels granted his request, so Lot headed towards Zoar. The Scripture says Lot arrived in Zoar just moments before sunrise. "But Lot's wife looked back, and she became a pillar of salt." (Gen. 19:26)

A Curious Quandary

After reading this story, it is hard to resist asking another question. "Why did Mrs. Lot look back?" Well, the writer of Gill's Exposition of Luke 17:32 surmises that, she wanted to see what had happened to her birthplace, her father's house, and all her neighbors.

Fate, Fancy and Folly

She wanted to see the fate of her hometown. She was overly attached to the stuff she was leaving behind. She also had a fancy for the life she was walking away from. Besides, she was unsettled about her future in the small town of Zoar.

Heartsick Over Sodom

Although she was rescued from the destruction that doomed her cursed city, Mrs. Lot was still heartsick over Sodom. So just when the gleaming glow of sunrise streamed above the horizon, Mrs. Lot stopped, turned around, and took one last look. That one last look sealed her fate and earned herself a place in infamy and history. Evidently, God was very displeased with her action. Consequently, He turned her into a monument of disbelief, distrust and doubt.

Due to the passing of time, and the absence of a confession from Mrs. Lot, it's almost impossible to discern the real reason for her hankering gesture. Nevertheless, the real reason Mrs. Lot looked back is a minor matter in this discussion. Our immediate concern should not be deducing the real reason MRS. Lot looked back. Instead, our focus should on the Lord's admonition for us today. "Remember Lot's wife!" Why? Well for one thing, it appears Lot's wife did not fully realize the personal effort heaven had made to ensure her personal safety and that of her family.

success of a daring rescue mission of herself and her loved-ones.

Sorrowful Over Ruins

Perhaps she was more concerned about her past and less about her future. She was lamenting the loss of her possessions, and discounting the value of her salvation. Seemingly, she was so preoccupied with the fate of sin city; she could not see the opportunities of a new start and destiny.

Evidently, Mrs. Lot was so accustomed to her life of ease in Sodom, she could not envision the Lord's provisions for her future welfare. Ironically, she was rescued, yet she felt like a captive. She was privileged, yet she felt deprived. She was blessed, yet she felt cursed. She was saved, yet she felt lost. She was highly favored, yet she felt terribly disfavored.

Conclusion

So the lesson for us today is, *we* must be careful not to repeat Mrs. Lot's mistakes. Jesus wants us to learn from her failings, and avoid her fate. The Lord wants us to remember her story, so we will never risk losing eternity for the comforts of our earthly homes.

Like Mrs. Lot, the devil wants to destroy us, but God wants to save us. Satan wants to ruin us, but God wants to rescue us. The evil one wants to keep us in bondage, but Christ wants to liberate us, redeem us, and restore our divine status in the kingdom of God.

Even now, the tempter wants to keep us guilt-ridden, but Jesus is saying to us, 'You are forgiven!' Indeed, the devil seeks to orchestrate the damnation of our souls. Thankfully, Jesus came to offer us salvation and secure our redemption. So there is wisdom in the divine admonition: "Remember Lot's Wife!"

We must never forget that God is our father, who loves us unconditionally, unreservedly and wholeheartedly. As our loving father, he has promised never to leave us or forsake us. We must remember that whatever we've given up, God can replace it. Whatever is taken from us, God can give it back. Whatever we've lost, God can restore it. Whatever we've left behind, God has something better in-store for us.

Today, Christ wants us to remember, He is our friend, when we are friendless. He is our help when we are helpless. He is our wealth when we are penniless; he is our new beginning, when we have lost everything.

Christ is our security in times of uncertainty; he is our hope amidst melancholy, misery and worry. The message for every reader today is to learn a lesson from Mrs. Lot's experience. When faced with life's worst emergency, it is important for us to recognize the divine rescue mission, and accept heaven's intervention to ensure our safety and security. We should never forget that Christ is able to establish our present, safeguard our future, and secure our eternal destiny. Knowing this, we can trust Him today, tomorrow and always.

The Last Word

> "Fear not; for I am with you: be not dismayed; for I am your God: I will strengthen you; yea, I will help you; yea, I will uphold you with the right hand of my righteousness." (Isa. 41:10).

Let us pray.

Heavenly Father! Thank you for your encouraging words; for reminding us of your loving intentions towards us. It is good to know you want to rescue us, save us, and lead us to a better place.

Lord, help us to learn from Mrs. Lot's experience; so we can avoid her mistakes. Give us the faith we need to trust you with our lives and our future. Teach us how to depend on you for guidance, for divine direction, and our daily provisions.

Lord, lead us from here to where we should be. Lead us from the present to the future; from our place on earth to our eternal home. Bless us today and always; we ask these favors in Jesus name, .amen.

Trust

Introduction

Are you a trusting person? Is there someone in your life you consider a trusted friend? Who is the most trustworthy person you know?

In the English language, some of the simplest words have the most complex definitions and usage variations. The word trust comes to mind as a good example of this. Generally, the word trust can have different grammar functions in English sentences.

At times, trust is an adjective, other times, a noun. It can even take the form of a verb. In this presentation, I will share a new perspective on this familiar, but important word—trust.

Defining Trust

Most English dictionaries define the word <u>trust</u> as confidence in someone or thing; to exercise strong faith in the pledge or promise of a person. It is dependence or reliance on the ability, integrity and surety of someone or thing; to count on or expect a predictable outcome.
https://www.dictionary.com/browse/trust?s=t

Public Trust

This simple, five letter noun is actually a big deal. It's a word we hear a lot about almost every day. Normally, broadcast-media like radio and television stations are portrayed as mediums of public trust.

The editors of print-media like newspapers, news magazines and journals make earnest efforts to engender trust in their readers. Manufacturers invest billions of dollars creating catchy slogans and appealing sound-bites to inspire consumers' trust in their products and services. Clearly, their company's image is shaped by the perceived prestige associated with their products and the supposed reputation of their top brands.

Corporate Trust

Companies large and small strive to create positive images in hopes of winning their clients' trust. Corporations and multinational firms sponsor art exhibits, cultural performances, and social events in order to portray themselves as good corporate citizens. In their view, trust is the commodity that enables them to gain market-share and attract investors.

By linking their company logo with popular events, they promote themselves as organizations deserving of the public's trust. Banks, financial and investment firms print brochures and posters, in which they highlight high-yield accounts and favorable projected returns on various investment options for depositors or investors. Such promotions are designed to inspire confidence in their current customers, and attract new ones.

Engendering Trust

Insurance companies like **All State**, **Met Life**, and **Prudential** are in the business of providing customers assurances of coverage in times of personal distress or crises. They also provide other valuable services like risk management, and financial safeguards that engender trust. Such insurers make institutional pledges to their customers and business clients, bolstering their confidence and security, even in times of uncertainty. Hence, whenever unexpected emergencies occur, and these companies keep their promises, their image of trustworthiness is reinforced, reaffirming customers' confidence in their companies.

Voters' Trust

During campaign season, many politicians compete for the same public offices. Each of them appears at political rallies, makes impassioned speeches, and promotes their ideas for solving the nation's problems. Since politicians are prone to make promises they are incapable of keeping, trust is often the critical factor that separates winners from losers.

In order to win voters' trust, they must provide more than feel-good rhetoric. Candidates who are able to articulate their constituents' collective concerns have a greater chance of being elected. Their abilities to articulate voters' dreams, hopes, and shared vision for their cities, counties, provinces and nations, enhance their chances of winning supporters' trust.

The Trust Principle

Ironically, the trust principle is equally important to academics and professional educators. Since there are thousands of schools, colleges and universities, students have many options to choose from. Knowing this, elite schools and Ivy League institutions invest both financial and intellectual resources; build state-of-the-art facilities, equipped with advanced learning tools and technologies in order to foster an enviable reputation and prestigious branding of their names.

In so doing, they create the perception that their campus is the best place to get a world-class education. Consequently, students are willing to make all the necessary sacrifices to gain acceptance into Brown, Cambridge, Columbia, Cornell, Dartmouth, Harvard, MIT, Northwestern, Oxford, Pennsylvania State, Princeton, Stanford, and Yale Universities.

Accompanying their efforts to attain and retain their superior status, these institutions invariably convey this

125

message to parents. "Trust us with your brightest and smartest youngsters. We will equip them with the right skills, develop their talents and intellectual faculties to achieve their dreams, become successful entrepreneurs, innovators, pioneers of industries, trendsetters in academics, business, politics, and social enterprises." This strategy is so effective, the best and brightest students from around the world submit applications during recruiting season, hoping for their chance to study at these schools.

Sacred Trust

Naturally, religious institutions are also considered bastions of sacred trust. By virtue of their profession, bishops, evangelists, imams, monks, pastors, preachers and priests not only encourage trust; they portray themselves as purveyors of divine authority. Hence, many regard them as ordained by heaven to induct congregants into a trusting relationship with God.

The biblical view of trust is closely linked with God's devotion and affection for mankind. This is evident in Solomon's admonition, "Trust in the Lord with all your heart, lean not on your own understanding. In all your ways, acknowledge him, and he will direct your path." (Prov. 3:5)

Trust in Divine Power

Dear reader, God wants to have a trusting relationship with us. Indeed, He longs to prove Himself to us as a trustworthy father, defender, protector and provider. The Lord knows that fulfilling relationships thrive on mutual devotion, respect and trust. Reality teaches us that life is full of dilemmas, dramas and traumas, tough choices and countless quandaries. Most often, it is difficult to know which decision is best, which option is most suitable, and which path will lead us towards the most desirable outcome.

Knowing this, some people turn to fortunetellers and palm readers. Others rely on horoscopes, psychics, and Ouija Boards. But the clever person trusts in the only wise God. Some people put their trust in higher education; others trust in financial institutions. Then there are those who put their trust in business tycoons, celebrated entrepreneurs, famous celebrities, socialites, industrialists, and investment gurus. But the prudent person trusts in the Lord of the past, present and the future. He alone is absolutely trustworthy—deserving of our trust.

Sadly, many people seem to have trust misplacement issues. How so? Well, they often put their trust in the wrong person or company, politician or organization. Some employees put their trust in the companies they work for—Arthur Andersen, Enron, Theranous, and World Com, only to be betrayed by crooked CEOs who mismanage their companies into corporate failures.

Some investors put their trust in financial institutions like Bear Sterns, Leman Brothers and MF Global. Then there are those who put their trust in pseudo financial gurus like Bernard Maddof , R. Allen Stanford and Russell Wasendorf Sr. This makes the Psalmist's observation a sobering assertion. "Some trust in chariots, and some in horses; but we trust in the name of the Lord our God." (Psalm 20:7)

In another passage, the Scripture encourages us in this manner. "Commit everything you do to the Lord; trust in him, and he will help you." (Psalm 37:5) Echoing the Psalmist, Solomon wrote, "Commit to the Lord whatever you do, and your plans will succeed. (Prov. 16:3)

A Trusting Relationship

Now, you may be wondering, how does one develop a trusting relationship with God? The answer is very simple. The same way a child learns to depend upon the parents to protect and provide for his or her needs, believers can learn to rely on God for his grace, lovingkindness and providential care. Most well-balanced children are confident about their parents' ability to ensure their wellbeing. Each time the child is comforted and nurtured by the parents' attentive care, a strong sense of belonging is confirmed, and a trusting relationship is reinforced and strengthened.

Consider this! Belief is the nutrient-rich soil in which faith grows. Likewise, faith is the nursery in which trust develops and thrives. Hence, trust is the firm belief fostered by faith. Indeed, we can only trust the person we believe in. Incidentally, trust is an integral part of the fledgling relationship between parents and children.

Childlike Trust

Starting with the first few years of my sons' lives, their strong attachment to me made my efforts to leave home alone an exercise in stealthy departures. When they noticed me getting dressed, they naturally expected to accompany me on my outing. When dodging them was not an option, their disappointed cries at the door made me feel guilt-ridden and remorseful. Though they had no idea where I was going, or what I would do there, they naturally wanted to be with me. Why? That's because they felt confident that wherever I take them, they would be properly cared for. Evidently, they felt assured that I would do my utmost to ensure their wellbeing on my outing as I do at home. Such assurance is evidence of trusting faith flourishing in tandem with their development.

Moved by their cries, I often relented, and take them with me. Then, once they got comfortable in their stroller or car seats, they would fall asleep shortly after leaving the house. Such child-like assurance of their well-being in my presence epitomizes the kind of trust-relationship we should strive to cultivate with God.

Fostering Trusting Faith

Starting with Eve's deception in Eden, the serpent incited our first parents' distrust in God—their divine caretaker. Gradually, the concept of distrust became a bane for the beings who bear God's likeness. Surreptitiously, the seeds of distrust were planted with the intriguing pronouncement.

Genesis 3:4&5

> "You shall not surly die. 5For God does know that in the day you eat thereof, then your eyes shall be opened, and you shall be as gods, knowing good and evil."

Sadly, during the past millennia, the seeds of distrust have been bearing a perpetual harvest of baleful fruits. Hence, mankind has developed a strong aversion to trusting in God. Actually, most of us are very disinclined, hesitant and reluctant about putting our trust in God's providential care. Consequently, the tendency to doubt, question and speculate on the certainty of God's word seems to increase with each generation.

Most often, evidence of our distrust usually manifest itself in disbelief. Such unbelief will, in time, inevitably reveals itself in our attitude towards divine instructions. Nevertheless, God is still desirous of fostering trusting faith in every believer. He tells us in the set of laws recorded in the books of Moses.

Deuteronomy 6:1-6

> 1Now these are the commandments, the statutes, and the judgments, which the LORD your God commanded to teach you, that you might do them in the land where you go to possess it: 2That you might fear the LORD your God, to keep all his statutes and his commandments, which I command you, and your son, and your son's son, all the days of your life; and that your days may be prolonged. 3Hear therefore, O Israel, and observe to do it; that it may be well with you, and that you may increase mightily, as the LORD God of your fathers has promised you, in the land that flows with milk and honey. 4Hear, O Israel: The LORD our God is one LORD: 5And you shall love the LORD your God with all your heart, and with all your soul, and with all your might.

Dear reader, God knows that learning to trust Him is not easy. Even so, you should also know that trust is like a cohesive force at the center of every fulfilling, growing and rewarding relationship. Indeed, it is impossible to serve God faithfully, unless we learn to trust Him completely and wholeheartedly. Certainly, such a trusting relationship may take years to develop.

Since our sinful nature frustrates our efforts to develop a trusting relationship with God, the process may be fraught with personal failings and spiritual struggles. Thankfully, God takes responsibility for our spiritual growth. Hence, He arranges events in our lives that provide opportunities to grow in faith, grace virtue, in favor with God and man. in faith, grace, and a trusting relationship with Him.

The truth is, our sinful nature conspires against any efforts to please God. Like wayward sheep, we are prone to wander away from God. Fortunately for us, the Lord, the Good shepherd comes looking for us. When he finds us, He picks us up, puts us on His shoulder, and carries us back to the fold of safety. Knowing this, we can take comfort in the Apostle Paul's assurance in the following statement.

> Being confident of this very thing, that he who has begun a good work in you will perform it until the day of Jesus Christ— (Philippians 1:6):

Pantheon Of Trusting Faith

One of the most reassuring themes of Scripture is the promises God makes to his people, and His faithfulness in keeping them. Most importantly, 'God will never abandon us, betray us, forsake us or break his promises to us.'

132

Instead, He will prove Himself trustworthy to us in unmistakable ways. Hence, the account of some Biblical heroes unwavering trust in God are object lessons for us today. First, there is job—the suffering servant, who trusted in God amidst the worst personal calamity anyone can suffer. Indeed, the exemplary way this patriarch dealt with his misfortune made him the object of affliction and adversity.

The story of Job's ordeal begins with a divine gathering of celestial luminaries. Surprisingly, Satan invited himself to that premier summit. Knowing Satan's knack for distressing the most pious people, God spoke of Job as "blameless and upright; a God-fearing servant who makes earnest efforts to shun evil." Hoping to prove that Job's faithfulness was fickle, and dependent on the blessings he received, Satan proposed a challenge. Boastfully, he vowed to cause Job to curse God by making his life extremely miserable and wretched. Next, Satan goaded God to remove his protective hedge from around Job. Signaling his confidence in his servant Job, God gave Satan full control over his family and property—(Job I:6-12).

Hearing this, Satan left the divine gathering, and immediately unleashed his destructive wrath on Job's family and all his possessions. First, the devil arranged a series of unfortunate events that resulted in the death and theft of Job's cattle. Knowing the bulk of Job's wealth came from the value of his prized herds, Satan gleefully waited for Job to curse God—(Job I:8-12).

Despite the tragedies that had befallen him, Job remained steadfast in his faith, and wouldn't even entertain any unfavorable thoughts about God. Ironically, Satan had proven Job to be as blameless and upright as God had said. That is, instead of cursing God, Job did the exact opposite. Distraught, but not completely despairing, Job tore his clothes, fell down and worshipped the Lord.

Job 1:21-22

> 21And Job said, Naked came I out of my mother's womb, and naked shall I return there: the LORD gave, and the LORD has taken away; blessed be the name of the LORD. 22In all this Job sinned not, nor charged God with wrong.

Thankfully, even after the tragic events left him childless, impoverished, disease-ridden, dejected and dispirited, his trust in God was unshakable. The truth is, Job was not immune to depression and despondency. Days later, Job's three friends went looking for him. When they saw him, they could not contain their anguished distress. Seeing him sitting in his grief-stricken state, they wailed in empathy for their compadre. Alas, after showing solidarity in their shared grief, they became judgmental and overcritical of their friend in his hour of anguish.

Feeling dispirited and downhearted, Job cursed his own existence, instead of cursing God. Overcome with sadness and sorrow, Job cursed the day of his birth, and the time of his conception. Then, he cursed the night, and even the midwife who first cared for him in his infancy. Later, after his friend condemned, judged and taunted him, Job lamented, "miserable comforters are you all"—(Job 16:2) Nevertheless, despite being subjected to immense and unspeakable suffering, Job emphatically asserted his innocence, and proudly defended his integrity.

Job 19:25-27

> 25For I know that my redeemer lives, and that he shall stand at the latter day upon the earth: 26And though after my skin is thus destroyed, yet in my flesh shall I see God: 27Whom I shall see for myself, and my eyes shall behold, and not another; though my heart be consumed within me."

Despite Job's steadfast faith in divine providence, there is no hint in scripture of God telling the patient patriarch the reason for his suffering. Nevertheless, the Almighty gladly commended his suffering servant, and appointed him intercessor for his friends' spiritual redemption. Indeed, Job's mediation on his friend's behalf was necessitated by their misguided and pompous pronouncements about the cause of his affliction. Even better, God rewarded Job for

135

his trusting faith by restoring his health, wealth and social status in his community (Job 42:7-11).

Job 42:12-17

> 12So the LORD blessed the latter end of Job more than his beginning: for he had fourteen thousand sheep, and six thousand camels, and a thousand yoke of oxen, and a thousand female donkeys. 13He had also seven sons and three daughters. 14And he called the name of the first, Jemimah; and the name of the second, Keziah; and the name of the third, Keren-happuch. 15And in all the land were no women found so beautiful as the daughters of Job: and their father gave them inheritance among their brethren. 16After this lived Job a hundred and forty years, and saw his sons, and his sons' sons, even four generations. 17So Job died, being old and full of days.

Actually, God does not always shield us from the trials and tribulations in this sinful world. Nevertheless, He stands ready to deliver us, protect us, redeem us, save us and uplift us. When we put our trust in God, He takes responsibility for our wellbeing. Indeed, God obliges himself to care for us, provides for us, does His utmost to ensure our safety, and prove Himself the trusted promise-keeper.

Even in times of uncertainty, we can be assured that God will prove Himself dependable, reliable, and trustworthy—deserving of our trust. Another noteworthy Bible hero that comes to mind is Abraham, a man who God said, "will command his own household after him." Next, is Moses, an exemplary model of humility, and "a friend of God." Then there is "Joseph, a man whose life exemplified the travails and triumph of a trusting relationship with God. ' See also 1 Sam. 26:9-11.

A Paragon of Faith

Unlike Job, Joseph, Daniel and his three colleagues, trusting-faith does not always lead to prosperity and triumph. Instead, our reliance on God's guidance and providential care may actually expose us to trials and tribulations. The Apostle Paul tells us plainly, "Yea, and all that will live godly in Christ Jesus shall suffer persecution—(2 Timothy 3:12). This unsettling fact was first conveyed by Jesus to his Disciples. "If they persecute Me, they will persecute you as well…"—(John 15:20). The truth is, they did more than persecute Jesus; they crucified Him in the company of two common criminals.

Like Paul, we are not called to a life of ease and luxury. Though material prosperity may be part of our present reality, our journey of faith will surely include some rough roads and troublesome times. Amidst such tumultuous treks, our reliance on God must hinge on our trusting-faith in the promises of his word. "I will never leave you, nor

137

forsake you"—(Joshua 1:5). Ironically, Saul was a prosecutor of Christians before his call to apostleship. Hence, when Christ summoned Ananias, and sent him as an envoy of the Fledgling Church, he had great misgivings about meeting the man who was persecuting the church. Responding to his objections, The Lord commanded Ananias in emphatic tone.

Acts 9:15,16

> 15But the Lord said unto him, Go your way: for he is a chosen vessel unto me, to bear my name before the Gentiles, and kings, and the children of Israel: 16For I will show him what great things he must suffer for my name's sake.

Shortly after his conversion, Saul, the persecutor became Paul, the prolific preacher and writer. Ironically, once Paul became a Christian, his fellow Jews started persecuting him. Throughout his ministry, Paul was harassed, hounded, and pursued by his former colleagues. Recalling his own tumultuous experience as the Lord's chosen vessel, Paul cited some of the harsh realities of his apostolic Odyssey.

2 Corinthians 11:24-26

> 24 Of the Jews five times received I forty stripes less one. 25Three times was I beaten

with rods, once was I stoned, three times I
suffered shipwreck, a night and a day I have been
in the deep; 26In journeys often, in perils of
waters, in perils of robbers, in perils by my own
countrymen, in perils by the Gentiles, in perils in
the city, in perils in the wilderness, in perils in the
sea, in perils among false brethren; 27In
weariness and painfulness, in watchings often, in
hunger and thirst, in fasting often, in cold and
nakedness.

When our trusting-faith in God becomes a bulwark of our
devotion, we, like Paul, can remain steadfast, amidst
afflictions, persecution and tribulations. Amidst the test and
trials that assail us, we can be assured that our afflictions are
opportunities to reaffirm our commitment to Christ. Years
before his conversion, Paul, formerly known as Saul,
pursued Christians, arrested them, brought them before
Jewish tribunals, to be tried sentenced, and stoned to death.
Shortly after his blinding encounter with Christ, his name-
change did nothing to shield him from persecution.

Once Paul started using his theological prowess to promote
the Christian gospel, he immediately became a high profile
target worth silencing. Still, knowing that his apostleship
was heaven-ordained, the risk of afflictions, beatings, death
threats, imprisonment, and martyrdom did not scare him.
Even when he was arrested and imprisoned, Paul used his
letters from lock-up to encourager the believers. Speaking
on behalf of timothy and other co-laborers, Paul used his

139

confinement to share a sobering exhortation with the Corinthian saints.

2 Corinthians 4:8,9; 16,17

> 8We are troubled on every side, yet not distressed; we are perplexed, but not in despair; 9Persecuted, but not forsaken; cast down, but not destroyed... 16For which cause we faint not; but though our outward man perish, yet the inward man is renewed day by day.17For our light affliction, which is but for a moment, works for us a far more exceeding and eternal weight of glory;

Despite his imprisonment, Paul did not see himself as a victim. Instead, he regarded himself the least of all the apostles, a mere co-laborer with Christ for the gospel ministry. Despite losing the respect of his former Pharisees, Paul made tremendous sacrifice for the Christian faith, without bemoaning his imprisonment. Notwithstanding his predicament, Paul invoked his trusting-faith in the Lord who called him on that Damascus Road. Finally, after years of preaching, teaching, writing his 14 epistles, and mentoring fellow ministers like Timothy, Titus and others, Paul recorded the most introspective, yet solemn sentiments of his divine calling and mission—his trusting-faith in the risen Christ and the gift of salvation.

<u>2 Timothy 4:6-8</u>

> 6For I am now ready to be offered, and the time of my departure is at hand. 7I have fought a good fight, I have finished my course, I have kept the faith: 8Henceforth there is laid up for me a crown of righteousness, which the Lord, the righteous judge, shall give me at that day: and not to me only, but unto all them also that love his appearing.

 Despite his afflictions and tribulations, Paul remained steadfast in his faith, trusting in the promises of God to secure his soul, even in martyrdom. That's the kind of trusting-faith every believer should develop, especially in times of adversity and afflictions. Those who strive to emulate the most noble virtues of Abraham, Joshua, Job, Daniel, Paul, and other paragons of faith, will learn to trust God in the good times and bad; amidst gladness and sadness, prosperity and scarcity. That way, we, like James, will learn to "count it pure joy when we encounter diverse *temptations* and trials"—(<u>James 1:2</u>).

Conclusion

Dear reader, God is not a philanderer; so your heart is safe with Him. It is unlike God to be a backstabber. So He will never betray your trust. The Lord is capable, dependable and reliable. So you can always depend on Him. Jesus is the friend who sticks closer than a brother. So He will never abandon you, never forsake you, never leave you alone.

<u>Isaiah 43:1&2</u>

> "Fear not: for I have redeemed you, I have called you by your name; you are mine. 2When you pass through the waters, I will be with you; and through the rivers, they shall not overflow you: when you walk through the fire, you shall not be burned; neither shall the flame scorch you."

When we learn to put our trust in God, we will discover that He alone is trustworthy—deserving of our trust. So you can trust Him with your finances; God pays the best dividends. You can trust Him with your family; His divine provisions will ensure the safety, security and prosperity of every member.

You can trust Him with your time; He'll reward you with eternity. You can trust Him with your life; He will lead you into a loving, nurturing, and trusting relationship with Him. You can trust Him with your future; He'll help you navigate your path to your eternal destiny. You can trust Him with your soul; He has secured your redemption, by paying the price for your salvation.

The Last Word

"Trust in the Lord with all your heart; do not depend on your own understanding. Seek his will in all you do, and he will show you which path to take." (Prov. 3:5&6).

Let us pray.

Heavenly Father! Thank you for the clarity of the Scripture, and a new perspective on the word trust. It is good to know you are a God we can trust. Give us the faith to believe in your words, depend on your promises, and put our trust in you.

Lord, we long to have a saving and trusting relationship with you. Reassure us with your trustworthy counsel. Enable us to trust you with our hearts, our lives, our plans, and our spiritual legacy. That way, you can secure our souls, and safeguard our place in your eternal kingdom. We ask these favors, in Jesus name, amen.

References

Websites Consulted

Anderson, Hans Christian. Web—Good Reads, 2013. June
28th http://www.goodreads.com/quotes

Moses, Grandma (1860-1861. Web—About Women in
History. Education. July 23rd.
http://womenshistory.about.com/od/quotes/a/grandma_mos
es.htm

Moses, Grandma (1860-1861. Obituary. Web—The New
York Times Company. July 23rd.
https://www.thoughtco.com/grandma-moses-quotes-
3530093

http://www.nytimes.com/learning/general/onthisday/bday/0
907.html

William Makepeace Thackeray Web—Good Reads Quotes
June 28th
https://www.goodreads.com/author/quotes/3953.William_
Makepeace_Thackeray

Youtube Video Clip. Paramount Pictures Presests Forest
Gump—July 23rd, 2017
https://www.youtube.com/watch?v=uWzrIX5l0vc

Malgorzata Chabrowska Web: International Coach—July 3rd, 2017 https://coachcampus.com/coach-portfolios/power-tools/malgorzata-chabrowska-attitude-vs-behavior/

Anonymous. Web—Oracle Thinkquest Education Foundation. Attitude and Behavior—July 23rd, 2017 http://library.thinkquest.org/C007405/attbeh/distatt.html

Sir **Winston Churchill** Web: Brainy Quotes July 3rd, 2017 https://www.brainyquote.com/quotes/quotes/w/winstonchu 104164.html

Personal Development Wisdom Web: Thomas Jefferson: Think Positive. http://personaldevelopmentwisdom.com/thomas-jefferson-think-positive.html

Zigler, Zig. Web—Quote Investigator—July 3rd, 2017 http://quoteinvestigator.com/tag/winston-churchill/

Inspirational Peak Web: Swindoll, Charles Our Attitude July 3rd, 2017 http://www.inspirationpeak.com/cgi-bin/stories.cgi?record=91

 Quotations Book Web: Quote of the Day, Dean Jimmy July 3rd, 2017 http://quotationsbook.com/quote/5662/#sthash.KZymRQ46 .dpbs

Maya Angelou Quotes Web: The Guardian 15 of the Best
Quotes— July 3rd, 2017
https://www.theguardian.com/books/2014/may/28/maya-
angelou-in-fifteen-quotes

Your Story Web: Oprah Winfrey, Her Story July 3rd, 2017
https://yourstory.com/2015/01/20-best-inspirational-quotes-
oprah_winfrey/

Anonymous Web: Healthy Thoughts Inspirational
Quotes—Life. July 3rd, 2017
http://healthythoughts.in/2012/12/12/

It's Worth Quoting Web: Confidence Quotes—Hazlitt,
William. July 3rd, 2017
http://www.itsworthquoting.com/confidencequotes.html

AZ Quotes—Dickens, Charles; Web: Online Literature
Library—A Tale of Two Cities, Book 3 – Track of a
Storm—July 3rd, 2017
http://www.azquotes.com/quote/532006

http://www.literature.org/authors/dickens-charles/two-
cities/book-03/chapter-06.html

Achieving Your Life's Mission Web: Powell, John—July
3rd, 2017
http://www.achieveyourlifemission.com/quotes/display/cat
egory/Confidence

Live it Forward! Web: Ralph Waldo Emerson—July 3rd, 2017 https://liveitforward.com/quotes-unlock-full-potential/

http://people.virginia.edu/~sfr/enam315/waldoemerson.html

Camille Pissarro Quotes. Web:camillepissarro.org—July 4th, 2017 http://www.camillepissarro.org/camille-pissarro-quotes.jsp

Elizabeth Bibeaso   Web: Elizabeth Bibesco Quotes—July 4th, 2017 https://www.brainyquote.com/quotes/quotes/e/elizabethb12 1464.html

Meltzer, Bernard. Web—Quotations Book—July 3rd, 2017 http://quotationsbook.com/quote/16935/#sthash.hSV4j3CC.dpbs

Carlyle, Thomas Web: Enotes Past and Present Quotes— July 3rd , 2017 https://www.enotes.com/topics/past-present/quotes

http://www.online-literature.com/thomas-carlyle/past-and-present/34/

Addison, Joseph. Web—Brainy Quote–July 4th, 2017 https://www.brainyquote.com/quotes/quotes/j/josephaddi14 8371.html

http://www.quoteland.com/topic/Contentment-Quotes/582/

Cohen, Alan. Web—Quotes on Gratitude—July 4th, 2017
http://awakenthegreatnesswithin.com/52-inspirational-quotes-on-gratitude

Nelson, Willie. Web—Brainy Quotes—July 4th, 2017
https://www.brainyquote.com/quotes/quotes/w/willienels38
1960.html

Jackson, Jesse. Web—Brainy Quote—July 4th, 2017
https://www.brainyquote.com/quotes/quotes/j/jessejacks38
5104.html

Dennis Waitley Web: Healthy Inspiration by Spark
People—July 4th, 2017
http://www.sparkpeople.com/resource/quotes_translation.as
p?id=446

McCarty, Hanoch. Web—The Quote Garden. July 3rd,
2017 http://www.quotegarden.com/confidence.html

Garvey, Marcus. Web—Brainy Quotes, Marcus Garvey—
July 4th, 2017
https://www.brainyquote.com/quotes/quotes/m/marcusgarv
365155.html

http://jamaica-
gleaner.com/gleaner/20130707/news/news4.html

http://sourcesofinsight.com/confidence-quotes/

Buddha Web: Famous Quotes and Sayings—July 4th, 2017
http://www.quotes.net/quote/3502

Socrates Web-IZ Quotes—July 4th, 2017
http://izquotes.com/quote/351571

Tzu, Lao. Web: Habits for Wellbeing Quots by Lao Tzu
July 4th, 2017   http://www.habitsforwellbeing.com/20-
inspiring-quotes-from-lao-tzu/

http://www.inspirationalquoteslist.net/

Unknown Proverb.   Web—Search Quotes—July 24th, 2017
http://www.searchquotes.com/quotation/221784

http://www.searchquotes.com/quotation/

John Balguy Web—Notable Quotes—July 24th, 2017
http://www.notable-
quotes.com/c/contentment_quotes_ii.html

http://www.worldofquotes.com/topic/contentment/2/index.
html

English Proverb. Web: Board of Wisdom—July 24th, 2017
http://boardofwisdom.com/togo/Quotes/ShowQuote/

http://www.scribd.com/doc/6675776/English-Proverbs-and-Oneliners

Buddha Quotes Web: Brainy Quotes—July 24th, 2017
https://www.brainyquote.com/quotes/quotes/b/buddha140966.html

http://www.quoteworld.org/quotes/2049

Anatole France Quotes Web: Brainy Quotes—July 4th, 2017
https://www.brainyquote.com/quotes/quotes/a/anatolefra161340.html

Barbara Johnson Web: AZ Quotes—July 4th, 2017
http://www.azquotes.com/quote/592846

http://www.inspirational-quotations.com/faith-quotes.html

Ralph Waldo Emerson Web: David Brim 13 Excellent Quotes—July 4th, 2017
http://www.davidbrim.com/dreamer-quotes/

http://www.quotesdream.com/quotesondreams_top100.html

Liam James Quotes Web: Liam AZ Quotes—July 4th, 2017 http://www.azquotes.com/quote/636301

Block, Lawrence. Web: Search Quotes, Dreams—July 4th, 2017 http://www.searchquotes.com/quotation/

Dan Zadra Web: The Quote Garden—July 4th, 2017 http://www.quotegarden.com/be-great.html

Karen Ravn Web: Famous Quotes & Sayings—July 4th, 2017 http://www.quotes.net/quote/16853

Donne, John. Web: To the Countess of Bedford—July 5th, 2017
http://www.luminarium.org/sevenlit/donne/bedford1.htm

https://www.saveaquote.com/quotes/life/quote-334176

Sherwood Eddy Web: Brainy Quotes—July 5th, 2017 http://www.brainyquote.com/quotes/quotes/s/sherwooded105072.html

Henry David Beecher Web: IZ Quotes on Faith—July 5th, 2017 http://izquotes.com/quote/14556

Clark, William Newton. Web: Search Quotes—July 5th, 2017 http://www.searchquotes.com/quotation/

Christian Nestell Bovee Web: Brainy Quotes—July 5th, 2017

https://www.brainyquote.com/quotes/authors/c/christian_ne
stell_bovee_2.html

Carroll, Ramona C. Web: Board of Wisdom Faith
Quotes—July 5th, 2017
http://boardofwisdom.com/togo/Quotes/ShowQuote?msgid
=136111#.WVxLiONuKUl

http://www.finestquotes.com/select_quote-category-Faith-
page-1.htm

Gill, John. Web—Exposition of the Entire Bible July 26th.
http://biblehub.com/genesis/19-26.htm

Russell R. Wasendorf Sr.
https://archives.fbi.gov/archives/omaha/press-
releases/2013/peregrine-financial-group-ceo-sentenced-to-
50-years-for-fraud-embezzlement-and-lying-to-regulators

Bernie Madoff https://www.businessinsider.com/how-
bernie-madoffs-ponzi-scheme-worked-2014-7

R. Allen Stanford
https://www.nytimes.com/2012/06/15/business/stanford-
sentenced-to-110-years-in-jail-in-fraud-case.html

Other Works by the same Author

<u>Below is a sample list of op-ed articles published in Korean English Dailies.</u>

The Best News Ever! Web: The Seoul Times
http://theseoultimes.com/ST/?url=/ST/db/read.php?idx=135 07

Gift-giving and Christmas Web: The Seoul Times
http://theseoultimes.com/ST/?url=/ST/db/read.php?idx=135 07

Not Again! Web: The Seoul Times
http://theseoultimes.com/ST/?url=/ST/db/read.php?idx=135 07

A Memorable Chuseok Web: The Seoul Times
http://theseoultimes.com/ST/?url=/ST/db/read.php?idx=135 07

Cherishing Our Children Web: The Seoul Times
http://theseoultimes.com/ST/?url=/ST/db/read.php?idx=135 07

Year of the Earth Dog Dawns Web: The Seoul Times
http://theseoultimes.com/ST/?url=/ST/db/read.php?idx=135 07

The Fire Rooster: Proclaimer of a New Reality Web: The
Seoul Times
http://theseoultimes.com/ST/?url=/ST/db/read.php?idx=135
07

Start of Something New Web: The Seoul Times
http://theseoultimes.com/ST/?url=/ST/db/read.php?idx=135
07

A day for expressing love Web: Korea Times— 2012-02-
13 http://www.koreatimes.co.kr/www/news/opinon/2012/0
7/162_104732.html

In Retrospect Web: Korea Times—2011-12-30
http://www.koreatimes.co.kr/www/news/opinon/2012/07/1
62_101928.html

An Auspicious Year Web: Korea Times——2012/07
http://www.koreatimes.co.kr/www/news/opinon/2010/02/1
37_60887.html

Commerce & Christmas Web: Korea Times—2009/08/27
http://theseoultimes.com/ST/?url=/ST/db/read.php?idx=873
3

http://mengnews.joins.com/view.aspx?aId=2909260

Ban Ki Moon English Contest Web: Korea Times—
2009/11/27

http://joongangdaily.joins.com/article/view.asp?aid=29129
30

One Year Later Web: Korea Times—2010-01-28
http://www.koreatimes.co.kr/www/news/opinon/2010/01/1
97_59865.html

An EPIK Excursion Web: Korea Times—2009-07-27
http://www.koreatimes.co.kr/www/news/opinon/2009/07/1
37_49156.html

An Exemplary Life Web: The Seoul Times
http://theseoultimes.com/ST/?url=/ST/db/read.php?idx=121
70

Honoring the Family Web: Korea Times—2007/05/29
http://www.koreatimes.co.kr/www/news/include/print.asp?
newsIdx=3214

Autumn's Festival of Colors Web: Korea Times—a
2007/10/23
http://www.koreatimes.co.kr/www/news/include/print.asp?
newsIdx=12409

Christmas at Odds with Christianity Web: Korea Times
http://www.koreatimes.co.kr/www/news/opinon/2008/04/1
62_15419.html

Discovering Stargazing Web: Korea Times—2007/12/25
http://www.koreatimes.co.kr/www/news/opinon/opi_view.a
sp?newsIdx=16135&categoryCode=162

Solace for late Actress Choi Jin Shil's Children Web:
Korea Times
http://www.koreaherald.com/view.php?ud=2013011300
0272

About the Author

Carlton U. Forbes is an educator, with more than two decades experience, teaching English as a second language in South Korea. During that time, he has taught communicative English to students in elementary, middle and high school. Additionally, he has also worked as an assistant professor of English Language and Culture at Hankyong National University, in Anseong, South Korea. Before joining HKNU, Mr. Forbes worked at Hannam and Woosong Universities in Daejeon, Pusan National University in Busan, and Dongyang University in Youngju City, North Kyungsang Province.

Currently, Mr. Forbes is a free-lance English language instructor, providing private students specialized English instruction. He also teaches individuals and small groups, as requested. Currently, Mr. Forbes is preparing a collection of ESL Task-Based Communicative Lessons for beginners and intermediate students.

Mr. Forbes entry into English language training (ELT) began in 1994, when he became a missionary-teacher in South Korea. While working at Sam Yook Language Schools, Mr. Forbes traveled throughout the Korean peninsula, lecturing, preaching, and teaching at academic and religious gatherings. Then, in 2009, Mr. Forbes joined the English Program In Korea, (EPIK), where he taught conversational English in North Chungcheong Provincial Public Schools. Much of his time with EPIK was spent at

Beak-gok, and Kwang-hye Won Middle Schools in Jincheon County, along with Sannam Middle School in Cheong-ju.

Mr. Forbes is married to his lovely wife Wanda, and, together they have three sons. He attended Oakwood University (formerly Oakwood College), where he earned a bachelor a Bachelor of Social Work BSW). Shortly after completing his studies, he joined the Adventist Volunteer Service, and was sent to South Korea as a missionary-teacher.

After laboring in the mission field for nearly a decade, Mr. Forbes enrolled at Adventist International Institute of Advanced Studies in the Philippines (AIIAS). He graduated in 2006 with a Master of Divinity degree. He is the author of two books: Task-Based Communicative English, and ESL Bible Handbook.

Aside from his lesson development and classroom presentations, Mr. Forbes enjoys creative writing, storytelling, and public speaking. While in Korea, he has written and published numerous articles on various topics in the Korea Herald, & Times; Joongang Daily, and the online daily, The Seoul Times (theseoultimes.com). Mr. Forbes also likes spending time in the great outdoors, bicycle riding, hiking, mountain climbing, rollerblading, and playing just about any sports his three boys are interested in.

Alongside his reading and writing pastime, Mr. Forbes enjoys traveling, and sharing his thoughts on various topics to eager audiences. His friends, colleagues and associates regard him as an enlivening lecturer, preacher, teacher, and a great thinker.

When planning your next event, consider booking Mr. Forbes to liven your camp meeting, graduation, youth retreat, revival, seminars, school assembly, workshops and other gatherings. He knows how to engage an audience with animating and interactive presentations. In fact, he seems to have a natural knack for inspiring, motivating, and stimulating everyone in his audience. Mr. Forbes can be reached at cuforbes@gmail.com

Made in the USA
Middletown, DE
22 August 2024

59010624R00095